The History of
St Peter's Church
London Colney

GW00707295

Kenneth Barker

Published by:
Kenneth Barker
64 Morris Way
London Colney
Hertfordshire
AL2 1JN

From whom further copies can be ordered

ISBN 978-0-9553114-2-0

Printed by
Print Resources
Welwyn Garden City

*Front cover adapted from a photograph by John Bassham
by kind permission of Jill Bassham*

I attended Lord Hardwicke this day...as to the project long in my heart...of a Chapel at London Colney...[and] I agreed for a site within the Parish of St Peters as the most eligible and only procurable site, though I should have prefer'd one within Shenley Parish.

Diary entry of Thomas Newcome, Rector of Shenley
1 May 1823

Other books by the author

SOUTH FROM BARLEY
The Story of the South Family
and
Samuel South & Sons

HOW RURAL TOTTENHAM DISAPPEARED

Contents

Foreword

Beside the River Colne in London Colney stands a little gem of a church called St Peter's and for six years I have had the privilege of serving God and the village community. This picturesque church was built 185 years ago and has earned a special place in the hearts of the community as a gathering place in sad times and in moments of joyous celebration.

Being beside a river the church attracts the attention of passers-by and since my arrival I have been frequently bombarded by questions, such as: *'who built it?*; *'how were the Caledon family involved?'*; *'what was the church like when it was built?'*; *'why do have you such a beautiful and grand stained glass window?'* and many others in similar vein. Sadly, there was no comprehensive history of the church to refer to and it became apparent that there was so obviously a need for it. So, to rectify this, the Parochial Church Council and myself decided to approach the author, Ken Barker, a resident of London Colney, and after two years of thorough research, the result is this wonderful book.

It is a book which is informative and highly researched yet still manages to be a captivating read. It highlights the struggles and machinations involved in the birth and continuing life of St Peter's Church. Where possible, each fact is verified with evidence sourced from archival records with much of the historical documentation coming to light for the first time.

As St Peter's prepares to re-order the present building in order to meet the needs of a new generation, the book inspires us to realise that our struggles, financial and otherwise, are nothing new but an integral part of the church history. Ken has written the definitive book on London Colney's Parish Church and in buying this book you too will be contributing to the continuing life of St Peter's.

Reverend Lynne Fawns
Vicar of St Peter's Church, London Colney
2010

Preface

It has been a privilege, as well as a rewarding experience, to research and write the history of St Peter's Church, London Colney. It is my hope that the resulting book will be a work of record for many years to come and that the sale proceeds will provide a useful contribution to church funds. Publication follows a tradition of fund raising in a similar manner. In 1825 Thomas Newcome, Rector of Shenley and promoter of a church in London Colney, donated the profits from the biography of John Sharp, Archbishop of York 1689-1714, to the building fund. One hundred years, later in 1925, the son of the minister, Thomas Bluett, wrote and published a short history of the church and district which was sold for the benefit of the Church Restoration Centenary Fund.

Ken Barker 2010

Acknowledgements

This book could not have been written without the assistance and co-operation of clergy and parishioners, past and present, together with other sources.

Particular mention should be made of the centenary booklet written by Thomas Bluett junior, the son of Thomas Bluett, vicar of St Peter's Church (1893-1927), and published in 1925. The booklet describes certain physical aspects of the church which are no longer visible and, not being mentioned elsewhere, would have remained unrecorded. More recent research has drawn on the modern archive and photographic record compiled by John Webb.

It has been a delight to discover that much archive material of the early days of the church has survived and grateful acknowledgement for their assistance is owed to the staffs at the Church of England Record Centre, Hertfordshire Archives and Local Studies, Lambeth Palace Library, London Metropolitan Archives and also the London Colney History Society.

Thanks are due to David Ansell; Judy Barker; Jill Bassham; Michael Beer; Richard Butler; Roger Collor; Emma Critchley; Mary Cook; Peter Dalling; Peter Darrell; Geoff Eldridge; Lynne Fawns; Ann Hansen; Margaret Hopkins; Marjorie Jackson; Pat O' Grady; Eric Pask; David Ridgeway; Maureen Ridout; Don Shortman; Jane Tompsett; Len Tompsett; John Webb.

With sincere apologies for any inadvertent omissions.

Sources

The intention of the book is to be a work of record with information taken from source material where practicable. Sources, where appropriate, appear as end notes to each chapter with the following abbreviations:

CA = Church Archive
CERC = Church of England Record Centre
HALS = Hertfordshire Archives and Local Studies
LPL = Lambeth Palace Library
LMA = London Metropolitan Archives

Notes

For the avoidance of possible confusion, it has been necessary to decide upon which of alternative descriptions are appropriate for certain of the topics included in the book:

- The foundation stone for the church was laid in 1824, construction was completed in 1825 and consecration followed in 1826. Following the example of the centenary booklet, 1825 is adopted as the founding date.

- Deliberation as to which description, church or chapel, was more correct at the various stages in the history of St Peter's Church was resolved by discovery of the following passage in 'The Law of the Building of Churches, Parsonages and Schools' written by barrister, Charles Trower, and published in 1867:

> How, then, it may be asked does a Church differ from a Chapel? It must be confessed that no satisfactory answer to this can be found in the text books; and as regards the C.B.A. [Church Building Acts], the terms Church or Chapel are not (as they should have been) defined at all, but are often used indifferently, and jumbled together, the one being used for the other, and sometimes the one or the other omitted where it ought not.

In the text, church and chapel are used as interchangeable descriptions.

- The church was described in the consecration certificate as St Peter Colney and is referred to as such in subsequent documents and publications although, on occasion, transposed as Colney St Peter. In 1998 the title was regularised as St Peter's Church, London Colney, (to distinguish it from the former mother church, St Peter's, St Albans) and is adopted as the nomenclature, as appropriate, throughout the text.

- For the sake of uniformity, Tyttenhanger (and not Tittenhanger) is used when referring to the local estate of the Hardwicke and Caledon families.

Currency	Before 1971 money is pre-decimal 12 pence (d) = 1 shilling (s) 20 shillings = 1 pound (£) No attempt has been made to convert amounts to present day (2010) values. Readers are recommended to visit www.measuringworth.com/ukcompare for a calculator (to 2007) and information on the different interpretations of comparative values.
Measurements	Of land are given in acres, roods and perches (or poles) 40 perches (p) = 1 rood (r) 4 roods = 1 acre

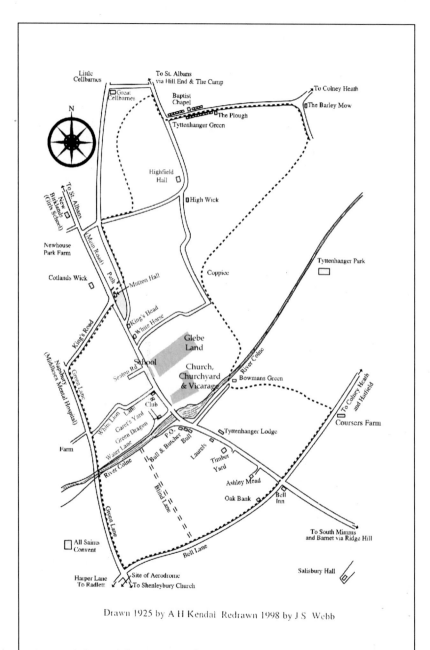

Drawn 1925 by A H Kendal Redrawn 1998 by J S Webb

Adapted from map appearing in Centenary Booklet

CHAPTER ONE

Introduction

In 1825, when St Peter's Church, London Colney, was built, George IV was on the throne and a Tory government under the premiership of Lord Liverpool governed a population of some 20 million in Great Britain and Ireland. The defeat of Napoleon at Waterloo 10 years earlier in 1815 was a recent memory and the Reform Act of 1832 lay 7 years in the future. It was not until 1830 that the Liverpool and Manchester Railway, the first public passenger carrying rail service, heralded the dawn of the steam age and journeys by horse-drawn coaches were the mode of transport used to travel the country. At that time London Colney was a rural community of a few hundred souls many of whom lived in dwellings clustered around the London to Holyhead road and the bridge built in 1774 to carry the thoroughfare over the River Colne. The prosperity of the village was closely linked with the ancient route which has been described as '*one of the most celebrated of all the roads out of London, as it carried nearly all the traffic between the metropolis and Liverpool, Manchester and Birmingham besides being the great highway to Ireland, by way of Chester and Holyhead...[and] the most important probably in the kingdom for the purposes of mail-coach travelling*'[1].

During the peak years of coach travel there were 26 inns in the village, typically arranged in pairs, providing refreshment and accommodation for travellers with the gentry receiving hospitality at one of the establishments whilst servants and coachmen were relegated to its neighbour. An 1832 advertisement for the sale of a property in London Colney includes the statement that '*70 coaches pass and repass daily*'[2]. From 1715 until 1873 the section of the road through London Colney was administered by the St Albans & South Mimms Turnpike Trust and the volume of traffic attracted the attention of highwaymen. Even John Churchill, Earl (later Duke) of Marlborough (1650-1722) and the victor of the battle of Blenheim, was relieved of 500 guineas whilst travelling near London Colney in 1692 by a gang thought to be responsible for other outrages[3]. A more favourable experience of the village was described in the memoirs of Sydney Owenson, Lady Morgan (1776-1859), a prominent novelist of her time, and published in

1

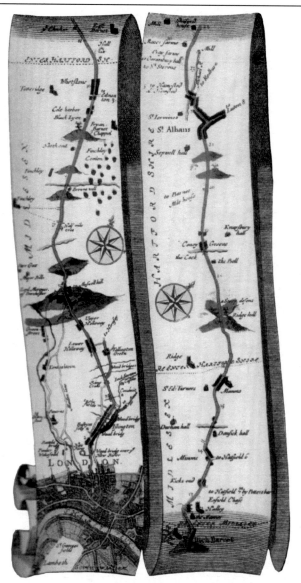

1675 John Ogilby road map
London to Holyhead (London to St Albans section)

1862[1] after her death. She writes of a journey by horse-drawn coach undertaken with her husband, Sir Charles Morgan, in 1835. It is worthwhile reciting her comments at length because they offer a glimpse of life in London Colney shortly after St Peter's Church was built and provide an introduction to the first minister of the church:

> July 21 – With a heavy heart, as with presentiment of the misery that awaited me. Even before leaving London, at seven in the morning, my dearest Morgan [husband] looked ill, and complained. At the end of the first stage he was taken ill – this was Barnet, and before we reached the second stage it was an interval of agony to both. He became very faint; I fanned and bathed his face with eau de cologne – it was very hot – and becoming fainter, he fell lifeless into my arms. As we were galloping down hill [Ridge] at the time, the carriage could not stop. At last we drew up at a little pot-house inn, the Black Bull [now the Bull], London Colney, where he was taken out of the carriage helpless, and thrown on a wretched bed.
>
> No medical aid nearer than St Alban's, four miles off; thither I sent. What an interval! His extremities cold; his hands blue; congestion coming on; I helpless, hopeless, watching all this!
>
> The arrival of surgeon Lipscomb – his active practice – covering him with hot tiles, mustard, blisters, bleeding him profusely, in a word saved his life – and mine. If there is desolation on earth, and misery in supreme helplessness, it is a situation in which I was placed. I dare not think of it.
>
> I discovered I was in the neighbourhood of Royal Porters[2]! And making my dreary position known to Colonel and Mrs White, they came to invite us to the great house; but this was impossible, so they supplied us with fresh flowers, fruit, and wine, and with the delight of my dear husband's hourly recovering under my eyes, I began to think the Black Bull a very lively place.
>
> I filled the little Sunday parlour with flowers, and heard the whole history of Mrs Black Bull, the hostess, and of her son, the butcher; and in the evening, when Morgan slept, I took my seat on a bench before the door with 'boots' (Sam Edgell) and 'mine host,' with a pot and a pipe on a round table before us, with such stories of highways and byeways! – a new view to me of humanity and society.
>
> Wayworn travellers stopping and economizing a few halfpence in the matter of refreshment – and the poor weary women - and the pleasure I felt in turning a pint of small beer into a pint of good ale, which was thought so noble on my part – and the joke cracked by

Sam, with the natty returning postilion – for little Sam, a rickety fellow of two feet and half high, the Asmodeus of the Black Bull, was evidently the wit *titre* of London Colney! Then the lovely, quiet scene, the pond and the stream, the parson's house; the cattle coming home, and the shower of red sunset showing over all! A gentleman in black passed us and took off his hat. Our landlady said, 'Tis our rector, who sent your ladyship the sal volatile and offers of services.'

Sydney Owenson,
Lady Morgan

The great skill and vigilance of Dr Lipscomb brought back my husband and life to me. In London he might have died for want of that close attention paid him by this country doctor. We have had more opportunity of becoming acquainted lately with this order of medical men. What talent in obscurity! What worth unknown! while charlatanism is fed and flourishes in this world, beyond all talent and all worth.

July 25 - While seated on the stone bench of the Black Bull, the rector approached me with a look of curiosity and doubt, and said he had heard of Sir Charles' illness, and he had come to offer his services to us both. He told me he was a Divine of two pluralities, the rector of London Colney[3], and something else that I forget, and while we sat gossiping before our cabaret, he said he could scarcely believe that the companion of Sam and the master of the Black Bull was Lady Morgan of whom he had heard so much etc.

> As the dew and darkness were falling we adjourned to the little sanded floor parlour and a pair of tallow candles, and talked of books and the fashions of the neighbourhood of London Colney. In short, my parson was a parson of gentility, and an agreeable man of the world.

During the 20th century horse-drawn transport gave way to motor vehicles and the Holyhead road became the A6 trunk road with the changing needs of travellers attracting petrol stations and transport cafes. The increasing volume of traffic passing through the village was relieved by the construction of a by-pass opened in November 1958[4]. Today, in 2010, the environment and economy of London Colney continues to be influenced by the proximity of the M25, M1, and A1(M) motorway network.

Until 1825, however, there had been no place of worship in London Colney and, despite the comments of Lady Owenson, the district was regarded as god-less rather than god-fearing. In 1823 the vicar of St Peter's Church (St Albans) wrote that '*London Colney being on the high London Road, and full of Publick Houses, exposes its people to examples and temptations, which must necessarily cause the Sabbath to be Lamentably neglected, or spent in an indecent and disorderly manner*'[5]. In evidence of these remarks a pillory and stocks[6], typically used for the punishment of drunkenness, were prominently positioned close to the bridge over the River Colne. The reputation of the locality lingered and some years later, in his Religious Survey of Hertfordshire of 1847, William Upton commented that '*Colney is a wicked place, with very few pious persons in it*'[7]. Several years of campaigning and fundraising were necessary before London Colney became the site of the first church to be built in Hertfordshire in the 19th century[8]. The efforts relied heavily on the support, financial and otherwise, of a large number of individuals but the Reverend Thomas Newcome and Philip, 3rd Earl of Hardwicke, merit particular recognition.

Thomas Newcome (1777-1851) embodied the virtues of enterprise, piety and service to others albeit from an assumed position of superiority. He was the ninth generation of his family to serve in holy orders. Born in 1777, the son of the Reverend Henry Newcome, Thomas studied at Queen's College, Cambridge, graduating with a Bachelor of Arts degree in 1801 and after ordination the same year he became the Rector of Shenley. The Newcome family had acquired rights to the rectorial tithes and in

Hertfordshire Archives and Local Studies

Circa 1840 Bridge over River Colne
(note stocks in fore ground)

Ken Barker

2009 The Bull Inn (formerly the Black Bull)

1835 the living was worth £1244 annually[9]. His ministry at Shenley was described by William Upton as *'Semi-Evangelical and very high Church'*. He married Charlotte Winter in 1806 and the union produced 10 children. In addition to his clerical duties Thomas Newcome was a magistrate, a member of the Barnet Board of Guardians, edited several books and established chapels of ease in London Colney (1825), Tottenham (1830) and Shenley (1840). Despite all of these activities Thomas Newcome found time to keep a dairy (or *'Family Register'*), now deposited at Hertfordshire Archives and Local Studies[10], which includes several references to the chapel at London Colney.

An inveterate letter writer to newspapers and magazines, one such published in 1834 (Appendix 2) describes his experiences in setting up the chapel at London Colney[11]. The campaign conducted by Thomas Newcome over several years to establish such a chapel is all the more impressive because his ecclesiastical responsibilities increased in 1824 when he was inducted vicar of All Hallows, the parish church of Tottenham, whilst retaining the Shenley incumbency. In his personal life, during the construction of the church, his bankers defaulted in November 1824 and his wife died in November 1825 after a long illness. Thomas Newcome died in 1851 aged 74 but his memory lives on with tolling of the bell at St Peters Church which is inscribed *'The gift of Thomas Newcome Rector of Shenley 1825'*.

The Right Honourable Philip Yorke, 3rd Earl of Hardwicke (1757-1834), enjoyed a distinguished career. He was Knight of the Garter, a Member of Parliament for Cambridge before his accession to the title in 1790, Lord Lieutenant of Ireland from 1801 until 1805, Lord Lieutenant of Cambridgeshire, High Steward of Cambridge University, Register of the Court of Admiralty and a Trustee of the British Museum. Landed estates in the possession of the Hardwicke family included the manor of Tyttenhanger which had passed to them through the marriage in 1755 of the first Earl to Catherine Freman, a member of the Blount family, the former owners. The manorial land at London Colney was leased on copyhold tenure and frustrated the first attempts of Thomas Newcome to acquire a site for the chapel that he was promoting. Copyhold was an early form of leasehold under which transfer of the tenancy required the copyhold to be surrendered to the Lord of the Manor and the new tenant admitted on the payment of a fine to the Lord although procedures were available to enfranchise the land converting the copyhold tenure into freehold ownership. Not only did the Earl provide a site for the new chapel and contribute generously to the building fund but also he became its patron endowing the annual sum of £40. Concurrently, he was the patron of the parishes of Foulmire and Wimpole in Cambridgeshire; Shenfield in Essex; Haresfield in Gloucestershire; Crudewell in Wiltshire; and Aspenden, Ayott, Ridge and Westmill in Hertfordshire[12].

Philip, 3rd
Earl of
Hardwicke

There were 4 sons and 4 daughters from the 3rd Earl's marriage to Lady Elizabeth Lindsay although, sadly, each of the sons predeceased him. The Tyttenhanger estate passed to his daughter, Catherine, who married Du Pre, 2nd Earl of Caledon in 1811, and thence into the Caledon family who continued as benefactors of the church and other establishments in London Colney over many years. Another daughter, Elizabeth, married Sir Charles Stuart (1816), later ennobled as the 1st Baron Stuart de Rothesay, and their daughter, Louisa, who became the Marchioness of Waterford, was responsible for the design of the Ascension window in the church. In 1925 Thomas Bluett junior, son of the minister, published a short history of the church in aid of the London Colney Church Centenary fund which was *'Dedicated by kind permission to The Countess of Caledon and The Lady Jane Van Koughnet'* suggesting that the costs of the booklet had been borne by them.

Descendants of Philip, 3rd Earl of Hardwicke

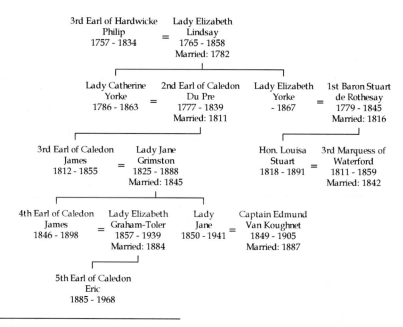

End notes

[1] Henry Law & S Hughes *Rudiments of the Art of Constructing and Repairing Common Roads* (John Weale) 1855 p 41

[2] The Times 18 July 1832

[3] Charles Harper *Half-hours with the Highwaymen* (Charles George) 1908 p 86

[1] *Lady Morgan's Memoirs Vol 11* Second Edition (Wm H Allen) 1863 p 399 et seq

[2] Porters Park estate in Shenley; later site of Shenley Hospital

[3] Erroneously described as 'rector', the Reverend Markham Barnard was the first incumbent of St Peter's Church and from 1832, became vicar of St Margaret in Ridge in addition.

[4] *The Times* 8 November 1958

[6] Erected in 1821 according the centenary booklet p 17

[7] *Religion In Hertfordshire 1847-1851* (Hertfordshire Record Publications) p 69

[8] Jeffery Whitelaw *Hertfordshire Churches* (Old Castle Books Ltd) 1960

[9] *Liber Ecclesiastical – An Authentic Statement of the Revenues of the Established Church* (Hamilton, Adams & Co) 1835

[10] HALS: Diary of Thomas Newcome Acc 2800 also published as *Two Nineteenth Century Hertfordshire Dairies 1822-1849* (Hertfordshire Record Society) 2002 (ISBN 0952377977)

[11] *The British Magazine & Monthly Register of Religious and Ecclesiastical Information* 1834 Vol III p 652

[12] *Patroni Ecclesiarum* List of the Patrons 1831

CHAPTER TWO
Founding the Church

During the early years of the 19th century there was pressure on the Church of England to adapt to the needs of a changing population and to counter-act a growing tendency towards non-conformity. Large numbers of people were moving from rural areas to the towns as the pace of industrialisation quickened and the existing parish system was unable to respond to the demand for new churches. These pressures resulted in the Church Building Act of 1818 accompanied by Government funding of £1,000,000 administered by Parliamentary Commissioners. Grants were made from the fund towards the building of churches in parishes containing a population not less than 4000 persons and not having either accommodation for more than a congregation of 1000 or where 1000 of the parishioners were residing more than 4 miles from any church or chapel. In the same year, the Church Building Society, supported by voluntary contributions and annual subscriptions, was established, alternatively known as the '*Society For Promoting The Enlargement And Building Of Churches and Chapels*', the organisation became the Incorporated Church Building Society in 1828[1].

There were similarities between the administration and operation of the 2 bodies with many of the Commissioners of the Parliamentary scheme serving on the Committee of the Society. The Commissioners, however, had the power to acquire land for a new church which was not available to projects funded under Church Building Society schemes but, otherwise, the erection of a new church was subject to the regulations of the Act. In order to demonstrate a need for a new church both organisations took into account the population anticipated to benefit; the proportion of free sittings to be provided; and the efforts made to raise funding from other sources. The rules of the Building Society[2] stipulated that no grant would be made '*unless the consent of the...patron and incumbent of the Church...already existing therein shall first have been obtained [Rule 14]*'; '*all parishes and places applying for aid shall state the extent of their population, their pecuniary means, and the efforts they have made, or are willing to make, towards accomplishing the object [Rule 16]*'; and '*...preference shall be given to such parishes and places as shall*

11

propose to afford the greatest extent of free sittings in proportion to the aid granted; such extent to be in no case less than half the additional area and accommodation [Rule 21]'.

The boundaries of 4 parishes converged at London Colney and it was the ambition of Thomas Newcome, Rector of Shenley, to build a chapel serving the inhabitants of London Colney within the boundary of his own parish which extended to the bank of the River Colne,. He later wrote '*I was once willing...& ready to build a Chapel at Colney in my Parish, without aid from any Society & without Endowment*'[3] but it was, of course, preferable if financial assistance was available from outside sources and the developments of 1818 provided such an opportunity. It is likely that he instigated the survey undertaken the same year into the '*Habitations in those parts of four Parishes which parts are nearer to London Colney than to any one of their respective Parish Church*'[4] which provided the following results:

1818 Survey				
Parish	Pop. nearer to London Colney[i]	Distance to Parish Church		
		miles	furlongs	poles
St Peter's (St Albans)	395	3	3	29
Shenley[ii]	289	1	4	0
Ridge	67	3	2	34
St Stephen's (St Albans)	166	3	6	0
Total	917			

[i] '*of which about ½ or more in the Village*'
[ii] *distance from the former parish church of St Botolph now a private residence*

The administration of the 4 parishes was:

Administration of Parishes				
Parish	Minister	Diocese	Archdeanery	Patron
St Peter's (St Albans)	John Briggs	London	St Albans	Bishop of Ely
St Stephen's (St Albans)	Francis Barker	London	St Albans	Alfred Fisher
Ridge	Jacob Jefferson	London	St Albans	Earl of Hardwicke
Shenley	Thos Newcome	Lincoln	Huntingdon	Thomas Newcome

The Population

in _____ Souls

St Peter's Parish	395
Shenley Parish	289
Bridge Parish	67
St Stephen's Parish	166
Total of the Population	917

Note. Colney Heath, in the Parish of St Peter containing a Population of 152 Souls is distant from St Peter's Church ... | m. f. p. |
from North Mims Church | 3 5 15 |
from London Colney | 1 7 2 |
| 2 0 10 |

Hertfordshire Archives & Local Studies

1818 Survey – map legend

The proposed chapel at London Colney did not qualify for a grant under the Church Building Act and Thomas Newcome approached the Church Building Society in July 1818 for further information[5]:

> I shall be much obliged to you for a copy of the Instructions to parties that may be requiring aid from the Society for providing the Enlargement & Building of Churches and Chapels and to state if there be any power given in the new Act of Parliament for the easy conversion of Copyhold ground into freehold; such proposed Chapel not being in a Parish that can be assisted by the Parliamentary Grant, but likely by its own efforts, as well as need, to merit the attention of the Society, if application be made, to it for its assistance towards building a Chapel of Ease.

He set about finding a suitable site in London Colney but, in the event, was unable '*to get any...eligible site within my own parish, all the land being copyhold; and if it had been freehold, there was not one...in the village that would have "freely" given land...*' A parcel of land was offered by Philip, 3rd Earl of Hardwicke, owner of the Tyttenhanger estate (and a vice-president of the Building Society), but the copyhold tenant was a '*stiffish dissenter*' who refused to relinquish any part of his tenancy declaring that '*...a church within*

13

fifty yards of the front of his farmhouse would annoy him as much as a meeting house would annoy me [Newcome] at the end of my parsonage garden!'[6].

There was the possibility of a site, again in the gift of the Earl of Hardwicke, within the neighbouring parish of St Peter's Church (St Albans) but Thomas Newcome, at that time, was not prepared to relinquish the control over the chapel which would inevitably result from such a relocation. In 1821 he wrote to the Church Building Society expressing his frustration[7] *'Your opinion was, not only that the case was out of the Parliamentary Grant and Regulations, but that there "was no power given by the Act, to enfranchise Copyhold Sites" that being the only Land within my Power – "except in such Cases, to which the Parliamentary Grant was applicable". Therefore I could apply to neither fund for this Holy and Patriotic Work!'*

He came to realise that in order to achieve his ambition he would have to forgo the earlier insistence that the chapel be established within his own parish of Shenley and a few years later the project was revived. His diary entry for 1 May 1823 records:

> I attended Lord Hardwicke this day & had many subsequent interviews & much Correspondence with Him, as to the project long in my Heart & first originating with Me (deo preveniente [with God's leadership]) of a Chapel at London Colney, and at his Lordships Expence [sic] of 150Gs [guineas - £157.50] I agreed (22d May) for a Site within the Parish of St Peters as the most eligible & only procurable site...

The proposed site that had been provided at a cost of £157.50 by Philip, 3rd Earl of Hardwicke, lay within the parish of St Peter's Church (St Albans) in which the greater proportion of the inhabitants of London Colney lived. Thomas Newcome knew that, in accordance with the rules of the Church Building Society (Rule 14), it was essential approval should first be sought from the incumbent and patron of the mother church in whose parish the proposed chapel was to be built before approaching the diocese and was later to write *'He [the Bishop] will not set up altar against altar, nor doctrine against doctrine, nor doctor against doctor; curate perpetual against the lawful pastor of every soul within the precincts of his cure, without very strong and manifest reason'*[8]. Accordingly he approached *'my friend and, ultimately, most hearty colleague'*[9] John Briggs, vicar of St Peter's (St Albans) who, in June 1823[10], wrote to the Church Building Society (Appendix 2) explaining his interest and confirming that the Diocese and Patron of his church were prepared to give their consent to the erection of a chapel within his parish at London Colney '... *a populous place; of which the greater part is in the said Parish and three miles and a half from the Mother Church; which moreover can afford no accommodation for its inhabitants; the remainder being in the Parish of Shenley and Diocese of Lincoln. Colney Heath, in St Peters Parish, is four miles from the Church and has a considerable population, scarcely within two miles of any Church'*[11]. He went on to explain that that a chapel *'capable of holding four or five hundred persons'* would suffice but *'There is, unfortunately, a heavy Church Rate levied at St Peters [St Albans] to pay Annuitants, who lent money 20 years ago for the re-building of the Church Tower and Chancel; and such generally, is the condition of the Inhabitants that nothing can be done Parochially.'*

In August 1823 a formal application[12] was submitted to the Society on behalf of the *'Earl of Hardwicke, the Rev John Briggs [vicar of St Peter's (St Albans)] the Rev Thos. Newcome [Rector of Shenley] and the Rev Jacob Jefferson [vicar of Ridge]'* on behalf of the *'Parish of Saint Peter , St Albans, Herts'* for aid towards the building of *'a Chapel at London Colney in the said Parish, and, collaterally, for the accommodation also, of certain Inhabitants of the Parishes of Shenley and Ridge in the same County.'* It was estimated that a population of 1000 would benefit from the erection of a chapel with accommodation for *'five or six hundred, if funds can be raised'* and providing free sittings from *'one third to one half of the population being very poor'*.

Approximately £300 had been pledged towards the costs but it was not considered that much headway could be made with fundraising until the possibility of a contribution from the Society was confirmed:

> The size & description of the Building must depend upon our success in obtaining subscriptions but it is imagined that from £1400 to £1600 will be required of which it is hoped that about 6,7 or possibly £800 would be collected privately, if the this Society should head the List, and patronise the undertaking

A grant of £400, payable upon consecration, was awarded by the Society subject to the condition that the chapel had capacity for a congregation of 750 persons with half of the sittings free of pew rents. The grant was recorded in the 6th annual report of the Society published in June 1824[13].

Considerable fund raising was necessary in addition to the grant and despite the church no longer being situated in his parish Thomas Newcome continued as the active promoter of the scheme becoming the treasurer responsible for canvassing and collecting subscriptions. He had misgivings, however, about the condition imposed by the Society and confided his thoughts in the diary entry for 18 August 1823[14] '... *the Condition annexed made the value of this Aid very problematical. A Smaller Chapel than 'for 800 Souls' would have sufficed...*'

Fundraising for the chapel was a daunting task but by May 1824, the sum of £1340 (excluding the £400 grant) had been either donated or pledged[15] (Appendix 3). Subscribers ranged across the spectrum of society from the landed aristocracy (Duke of Devonshire; the Earls of Hardwicke and Verulam) to Members of Parliament, clergymen, local dignitaries, professional men, tradesmen and persons of a humbler status including, surprisingly, a contribution from the recalcitrant non-conformist tenant who had expressed such strong opposition to the originally proposed site[16]. A donation of 1 guinea (£1.05) was made by the surgeon, Lipscomb who later treated Sir Charles Morgan during his illness at London Colney (Chapter 1). The largest subscriptions were made by the Earl of Hardwicke whose contributions (including the value of the church site) amounted to £357.50 and the lowest contribution was 1 shilling [5p]. In addition to his fundraising activities Thomas Newcome was also a contributor for £100. He was editor of a 2 volume book, *The Life of John Sharp, D.D. Lord Archbishop of York* [1691-1714] published in 1825 and expounded in the preamble that the motive for publishing the work was '*First and principally, to aid the founding a Chapel of Ease at London Colney in Hertfordshire, by appropriating the profit, if any, to furthering that object of his aim and wishes...*'

Concern continued to be expressed that the funding was insufficient for a chapel with the seating capacity imposed by the Church Building Society. In May, and again in August, 1824 Thomas Newcome wrote to the Society[17] requesting its agreement to reduce the number of sittings in return for a lesser grant of £300 because '*In the first place a Chapel for 600 would be sufficient for the present Population & future years may enlarge for themselves.*' He had become disheartened by the effort required to establish the chapel and threatened that unless *'the Society or the Parliamentary Board will kindly help or guarantee Me in some way I shall decline taking another step beyond advertising the subn [subscription] & the Reason of delay with my willingness to return all monies paid through my hands'*. In the event, the Society refused to alter its decision and Thomas Newcome, for his part, seems to have overcome his doubts and became manager of the scheme responsible for engaging and paying contractors.

George Smith (1782-1869) was appointed architect for the new church and provided his services without charge[18]. He was born in Aldenham and became a noted member of his profession being responsible for the design of several churches and other public buildings including the St Albans Court House and Town Hall[19]. In 1814 he became architect to the Mercer's Livery Company with which the first minister of St Peter's Church, Markland Barnard, and his father, had a close association. Invitations to tender were published in newspapers including The Times on 26 July 1824:

> To BUILDERS – Intended CHAPEL at London Colney, near St Alban's – The Committee for ERECTING this CHAPEL hereby give notice, that the plans and specifications will be left at the office of Mr Story, solicitor, St Alban's from the 12th to the 19th of July inst. and from the 19th inst. at the office of Mr Geo. Smith, surveyor, Bread-street-hill, London, for the inspection of persons who may be desirous of sending in TENDERS for the whole or part of the works. All the tenders are to be sealed up and delivered at the office of Mr George Smith, in Bread-street-hill, before the 2nd of August next. The committee does not pledge itself to accept the lowest tender but security will be required for the due performance of the contracts – July 7, 1824.

The identity of the successful tenderer has not been established but Thomas Newcome records in his diary that he set out the foundations on 14 August 1824 and a month later on 20 September 1824 the 3rd Earl of Hardwicke visited the site and laid the foundation stone.

Work progressed swiftly, by December 1824 the shell of the building was completed and the roof slated but the misgivings concerning the amount of money necessary to meet the seating requirements of the Church Building Society were then realised. There were insufficient funds to complete the project and further construction work halted. The Building Society grant of £400 was payable only after consecration of the chapel and pledges of further contributions were dependent on its continuing support. Thomas Newcome wrote to the Society in January 1825[20] reporting the position:

> The fabric is now covered in & it is much to be desired that Some one may be found willing to contract for paying for completion...all the money that has come or is likely to come into my hands is paid away or pledged & there remains therefore Nothing of a fund for completing the Chapel but the Society Grant of 400 upon Consecration. This I apprehend is not much above half the requisite Sum ...If the Committee should be disposed to appropriate another hundred pounds to this Chapel I think We may by great exertion get some further Subscriptions for finishing it.

On this occasion the pleas of Thomas Newcome were favourably received by the Building Society and its Committee agreed to a further grant of £100 again payable upon consecration of the chapel. The promise of the additional grant enabled fund raising efforts to be renewed and work on the chapel to be

LONDON COLNEY CHAPEL.—Subscriptions advertised up to May 10, 1824 - £1740 0 0

Subscriptions raised and collected since:

	£	s	d
The Hon. Misses Grimston -	20	0	0
His Grace the Duke of Devonshire - -	25	0	0
The Earl of Hardwicke, second subscription	100	0	0
— Burr, Esq Dunstable - -	5	0	0
J. P. Nares, Esq. Napsbury - -	10	10	0
The Rev. Thomas Snell, Salisbury Hall -	25	0	0
Thomas Portens, Esq. Colney Street -	5	0	0
Mr. Edward Harris, auctioneer, Barnet -	1	0	0
Mr. Douton, ditto, ditto - -	1	0	0
Mr. Hill, stonemason, ditto - -	1	0	0
Mr. White, draper, ditto - -	0	10	6
Miss Newcome, North Wales - -	5	0	0
The Rev. Thomas Newcome, second subscription to make 100l. - - -	35	0	0
Mr. Thomas Shirley, Salisbury Hall -	5	0	0
Captain Mason, R. N. - -	5	0	0
Rev. John Briggs, to make 50L -	25	0	0
J. Mico Winter, Esq. Shenley -	21	0	0
J. S. Story, Esq. law services, gratis -	20	0	0
George Smith, Esq. architect, by professional services and journeys, gratis - -	120	0	0
The Earl of Hardwicke, for books, communion plate, hangings for pulpit, desk, and altar, &c. -	105	0	0
The Rev. Thomas Newcome—Mr. Mears, the bell-founder's bill - - -	16	16	0
The Hon. Henry Pierepont, Tittenhanger -	10	0	0
H. M. Carter, Esq. Mayor of Hertford -	5	0	0
The Society for Promoting the Enlargement and Building of Churches and Chapels, by additional grant on consecration - - -	100	0	0

THOMAS NEWCOME, Treasurer.

List of Subscribers
County Herald 24 December 1825

recommenced. By December 1825 a further £570 had been subscribed[21], including further subscriptions from donors canvassed for a second time (Appendix 3), and the same month he was reporting that '...*the chapel has long been fit for consecration*'[22]. Other issues, however, had intervened to further delay the project and whilst these were being resolved the Church Building Society acceded to a request that part of the grant be paid. The sum of £400 was released despite the absence of a certificate of consecration.

The issues needing resolution were the status of the chapel and its minister; his financial support and accommodation; and the extent of the chapelry district. Each of the factors, to a lesser or greater extent, were inter-dependent and required the consent of the incumbent of the mother church. The failure to determine any one of them could impact upon the others and, possibly, cause the project to be abandoned. John Briggs had resigned the incumbency of St Peter's Church (St Albans) in 1823 and the possibility that his successor could be a less enthusiastic supporter of the chapel was foreseen by Thomas Newcome who wrote to the Church Building Society on 6 May 1824[23] commenting '*The Vicar of St Peters [St Albans] can know little of the matter, when he is inducted (Rev Briggs resigned some months ago) & we know not who is to be Vicar & in truth (conceit apart) He must come to me to know particulars & may be less friendly to the Measure than Rev Briggs was*'.

Until the enactment of the Church Building Act of 1818 the division of a parish by the creation of a separate ecclesiastical district required an Act of Parliament. At London Colney a district chapelry with parochial responsibilities administered as a perpetual curacy was envisaged comprising parts of the parishes of the mother church of St Peter's (St Albans), Shenley and Ridge described as '*All that district bounded on the north by Hill-end and Smallford, on the south by Shenley parish, on the east by Colney Heath, and on the west by Mapsbury (sic)*'[24]. With regard to the status of the chapel, in its simplest constitution a '*mere*' chapel of ease was '*built... for Divine worship, in aid or ease of the parish church, for prayers and preaching only, but in which a font is not allowed and the Sacraments (or at least the Sacrament of Baptism) and Burials not administered...and has no parochial rights, or endowment, or any territory of its own*'[25]. Conversely, a '*parochial*' chapel of ease was of a superior status and established with '*the rites of Christening and Burial...the true distinctive parochial features*'[26].

New churches and chapels established under the 1818 Act were created as perpetual curacies with the minister possessing a security of tenure similar to an incumbent vicar and superior to a stipendiary (or assisting curate) who was appointed and renumerated by (and remained in office at the pleasure of) the incumbent of the mother church. In further explanation:

> Perpetual curacies proliferated under the provisions of the new Acts, which gave this status to ministers of new churches of separate parishes, ecclesiastical districts, consolidated chapelries and district chapelries. Although such developments were commendable as far as they went, the first batch of Acts represented also a failure to grasp the larger and more fundamental issues of patronage, parochial reorganisation and clergy pay. It was to address this issue that new perpetual curacies were created, as safeguards against rectors, vicars and patrons who were fighting to retain their powers and their incomes, by blocking attempts to divide parishes with greatly increased populations.[27]

In further support of the enhanced status proposed for the London Colney chapel, Philip, 3rd Earl of Hardwicke, agreed to provide financial independence by settlement of a £40 annual endowment and, in addition, Thomas Newcome purchased a property adjoining the chapel site for the accommodation of the appointed minister[28].

By the time that Charles Norman was appointed the successor to John Briggs as minister of St Peter's Church (St Albans) in June 1824 he was faced with the creation of a separately endowed and distinct chapelry within his own parish having a significant degree of independence. The difficulties foreseen by Thomas Newcome were well founded because in April 1826 he was complaining to the Bishop of London '...certain it is that Mr Norman tardy consent to a District and his approval of the Deed of Endowment (making Lord H Patron and) reciting by way of preamble that His Majestys Commissioners had "reconveyed" (not cancelled) the Site and constituting Trustees has infinitely perplexed the Business'[29]. The letter had the desired effect and by July 1826 he was reporting 'Mr Norman having given his Signature together with my Lord Hardwicke, Archdeacon Watson the Vicar of Ridge and Myself to a Petition for the Consecration of Colney – Mr Barnard the Gentleman nominated Minister by Me, to whom Lord Hardwicke has kindly given leave to name his Presentee will this day lodge the Trust Deed, as approved *by Your Chancellor and the Petition with Messrs Shepherd Deputy Reg[istrar]'*[30].

On Saturday 15 July 1826, 7 years after the first approach to the Church Building Society and nearly 3 years since the foundations had been laid-out, the chapel was consecrated by the Bishop of London. The consecration brought the years of campaigning and effort by Thomas Newcome and his supporters to an end. He was able to request the Church Building Society to release the £100 balance of its grant and to provide them with details of the final cost[31]:

Building, furniture, consecration and Deeds of Trust	£2,800	-	-
Registrar's Bill (for consecration)	£45	-	-
Lawyer's Bill (for deeds)	£36	6s	6d

End notes

[1] Administration of the Society was transferred to the Historic Churches Preservation Trust in 1982 which was re-named National Churches Trust in 2007
[2] *The Christian Journal and Literary Register 1818* p 158
[3] LPL: Correspondence 6 May 1824 ICBS 00463
[4] HALS: annotated map D/ECd/P6
[5] LPL: Correspondence 24 July 1818 ICBS 00463
[6] *The British Magazine & Monthly Register of Religious and Ecclesiastical Information* 1834 Vol III p 652
[7] LPL: Correspondence 23 February 1819 ICBS 00463
[8] supra no 6
[9] supra no 6
[10] LPL: Correspondence 15 June ICBS 00463
[11] ibid
[12] LPL: Application ICBS 00463
[13] *The Christian Remembrancer* October 1824
[14] Dr David W V Weston *Ecclesiastical Law Journal* (Vol 5 No 23 July 1998) The Origins , Development and Demise of Perpetual Curacy
[15] *County Herald & Weekly Advertiser* 15 May 1824
[16] supra no 6
[17] LPL: Grant correspondence ICBS 00463
[18] *County Chronicle* 25 July 1826 p 2
[19] Howard Colvin *A Biographical Dictionary of British Architects 1600-1840* (3rd Edition) 1995 Yale
[20] LPL: Correspondence 12 January 1824 ICBS 00463
[21] *County Herald & Weekly Advertiser* 24 December 1825
[22] LPL: Correspondence 30 December 1825 ICBS 00463
[23] LPL: Correspondence 6 May 1824 ICBS 00463
[24] *Chapels belonging to the Church of England* (1842) W Clowes & Sons
[25] Trower, Charles (Barrister-at-Law) The Law of the Building of Churches 1867 p 7
[26] ibid p 8

[27] supra no 14
[28] CA: Indenture 30 September 1829
[29] CERC: Correspondence 7 April 1826 FP Howley 31 f 432r
[30] CERC: Correspondence July 1826 FP Howley 31 f 45r-45v
[31] LPL: Correspondence 1 September 1826 ICBS 00463

CHAPTER THREE

Chapelry, Parish and Patrons

The chapel of ease at London Colney was built in 1825 within the parish of the mother church of St Peter which was in the archdeaconry of St Albans and administered by the Diocese of London. In 1845 the archdeaconry was transferred to the Diocese of Rochester until 1877 when the bishopric of St Albans was created and the abbey church was elevated to cathedral status. St Peter's Church, London Colney, remains in the Diocese (and archdeaconry) of St Albans and, since 1987, is one of the 10 parishes that constitute the rural deanery of Aldenham. During 2010 the Aldenham Deanery will be dissolved and London Colney is preparing to become part of St Albans Deanery.

A separate and distinct ecclesiastical district was created for the new chapel and the boundaries were described by John Cussans in his History of Hertfordshire (1881):

> London Colney is an ecclesiastical parish only, carved in 1826, out of the civil parishes of St Stephen, St Peter [St Albans], Ridge and Shenley. In length it extends from the sixteenth mile-stone from London at Ridge Hill, to the One Mile House, midway between the nineteenth and twentieth mile-stones, on the same road; and in width from Napsbury, near Colney, to the Queen's Head, Colney Heath.

Each ecclesiastical office of the Church of England is the subject of patronage that was held historically by the person who had provided either (or both) the land for the church or an endowment towards the living. Such patronage conferred the privilege of advowson, that is to say, the right to nominate the incumbent for the approval and appointment by the diocesan bishop. Advowson could be transferred by inheritance or sale and in more distant times carried economic and political influence. Philip, 3rd Earl of Hardwicke (1757-1834), owner of the Tyttenhanger estate, was the first patron of St Peter's Chapel having given the site for the church also donating £200 towards the building costs, church plate and other furnishings together with an annual endowment of £40. He granted the privilege of nominating the first minister of the new church to Thomas Newcome, rector of Shenley, vicar of All Hallows Tottenham and promoter of the chapel, who recorded the

23

event in his diary on 10 December 1825, *'Lord Hardwicke. Having complemented Me with the Nomination of the first Minister. I named the Mr Markland Barnard of Trinity Coll[ege] Cambridge, Brother in law elect of Mr L[awrence] Gwynne my Tottenham Curate'*. At that time Markland Barnard had not been received into holy orders but in February 1826, upon graduation from Cambridge University, he was ordained deacon at St Mary-le-Bone Chapel, London[1] by the Bishop of Lincoln whose diocese administered the Shenley parish of his sponsor, Thomas Newcome.

Consecration of the new parish was delayed because the status of the chapel had been the subject of concern expressed by the recently appointed minister, Charles Norman, of St Peter's Church (St Albans), with the result that the endowment of Lord Harwicke was suspended. In the meantime, Markland Barnard was licensed as a stipendary curate of Shenley parish[2] at the instigation of Thomas Newcome who, in a letter to the Bishop of London[3], explained that *'I gave this gentleman a title to Ordination at the hands of the Bishop of Lincoln, with real intention to pay the Salary [£60] until he got the Chapel...'*. In the event that the obstacles to the creation of a chapelry district were not removed Thomas Newcome contemplated Markland Barnard remaining a resident curate of Shenley whilst administering the London Colney chapel on the principal that better *'half a Curate to a starved Minister'*[4].

Fortunately, the difficulties were resolved and on Saturday 15 July 1826, the chapel was consecrated by the Bishop of London, Dr William Howley with Thomas Newcome officiating as the Bishop's Chaplain. Amongst the congregation were the 3rd Earl of Hardwicke, patron and benefactor, Sir Christopher Robinson, Chancellor of the Diocese of London, Sir William Heygate, Alderman and former Lord Mayor of London, and clergy from surrounding parishes. After the ceremony the principal guests *'proceeded to North Mimms Park, the seat of Alderman Heygate...where they partook of a public breakfast, and thence returned to Stanmore Priory'*[5]. Within 2 years of his visit to London Colney, Dr William Howley was appointed Archbishop of Canterbury and officiated at the coronations of William IV (1831) and Victoria (1838). It was Archbishop Howley, accompanied by the Lord Chamberlain, who awoke the young Princess Victoria at Kensington Palace during the early hours of 20 June 1837 to inform her that her uncle had died and she was now Queen. In his earlier years, he was a tutor to the future 2nd Marquess of Abercorn and, thereafter, he continued to visit the Abercorn residence at the Priory, Stanmore, hence the reference in the report. In the 20th century the Priory achieved renown as the headquarters of RAF Fighter Command during World War 2.

The consecration was duly certified by the minister and the first appointed chapel wardens[6]:

> We the undersigned do hereby certify that St Peter Colney Chapel was Consecrated by the Right Honorable & Right Reverend the Lord Bishop of London on Saturday July 15th, in the year of our Lord 1826
> Markland Barnard BA Trinty College Cambridge
> Minister of St Peter Colney Chapel
> John Jaques Chapel Warden
> Thomas Barnett Chapel Warden

Five months later, in December 1826, Markland Barnard was licensed as perpetual curate of the chapel but concern about its status lingered. A few years later he was to complain that, after the death of the chapel warden, John Jaques, in 1834, his nominated successor, Henry Boome, on attending St Albans Archdeaconry, the *'Registrar refused to swear him on the ground that the Chapel at Colney being within the Parish of St Peter [St Albans] had no rights to have [a] Chapelry Warden but that the Church Warden of the mother church was competent to act'*[7].

The chapel was established with parochial rights but during the earlier years of the chapel it was the practice of the English Church to celebrate Holy Communion on Feast Days and selected Holy Days only. A return completed by the chapel wardens in 1834 declares that Communion was administered *'Four times'*[8] in a year; by 1842 the rural dean's Visitation Return reports an increase to *'6 times a year'*[9] and that there were between 35 to 50 communicants from an average congregation of 250 to 400. Eight days after the service of consecration at the evening service on 23 July 1826, John, the son of Frances and John Pridmore, a butcher, was the first infant to be baptised at the new chapel. The first burial service was conducted in June 1828 for William Pryor but it was not until 1838 that the chapel was licensed for the solemnisation of marriages.

The Church Building Act of 1818 stipulated that marriages could not be celebrated or solemnised in district chapels governed by the Act until after the '...*Death, Resignation or other Avoidence of the Spiritual Person who shall be the Incumbent of the Church of the Parish...*' [Clause 28]. William Leach had replaced Charles Norman as vicar of St Peter's Church (St Albans) in 1833 and following a petition from Markland Barnard and members of the congregation of the chapel at London Colney a licence to perform marriage ceremonies was granted by the Bishop of London in 1838 on the grounds that[10]:

> ... there is a population of at least six hundred and fifty Inhabitants residing in the immediate vicinity of the said Chapel and that by reason of their distance from the Churches of their respective Parishes or any Chapel wherein Marriages may be now lawfully celebrated according to Rites and Ceremonies of the Church of England they are subjected to inconvenience in the solemnization of their Marriages

Before the licence was granted it had been necessary to agree apportionment of the fees received for the conduct of marriages with the minister and parish clerk of St Peter's Church, London Colney, receiving '*the whole of the fees dues or other Emoluments so far as respects that portion of the district which is situate within the said Parishes of Saint Stephen and Ridge and one half portion ...so far as respects that portion of the said District which is situate within the said Parish of Saint Peter [St Albans]* '[11]. There was further provision that, at the time of the next vacancy for the post of parish clerk of St Peter's Church (St Albans), the whole of the fees would revert to the London Colney chapel. In a separate document[12] Thomas Newcome, as rector and patron of Shenley parish, together with his parish clerk consented to all of the marriage fees and emoluments being assigned to the chapel of St Peter Colney. On 26 November 1838, a month after the licence was granted, the Reverend Markland Barnard officiated at the marriage of George Fusedale, a tailor, to Susannah Halsey.

Two religious surveys undertaken in the mid 19th century provide a snapshot of the congregation attending St Peter's Church, London Colney, at that time. In 1848 a non-conformist minister, William Upton, produced his '*Statistics of the Religious Condition of the County of Hertfordshire'* which recorded 2 Sunday services (morning and afternoon) at the chapel with an estimated attendance of 200. Three years later, in addition to the decennial population census of 1851, an ecclesiastical census of places of worship of all dominations was carried out and has been described as '...*the only fully comprehensive religious census in the history of the Modern United Kingdom*'[13]. Although the census was voluntary over 34,000 returns were made including a response submitted on behalf of St Peter's Church, London Colney. The returns included details of the number of free and appropriated sittings, the number of attendances at each service on Sunday 30 March 1851 (actual and average attendances) and Sunday school attendances.

Duplicated returns were submitted on behalf of St Peter's Church. London Colney, and one form was crossed through by the Registrar with the validated return providing the following information:

Ecclesiastical Census 1851				
	Morning		Afternoon	
	Actual	Average	Actual	Average
General Congregation	140	150	450	460
Sunday Scholars	120	120	120	120
Total	260	270	570	580

The duplicated return provided slightly different information for the morning general congregation:

	Morning		Afternoon	
	Actual	Average	Actual	Average
General Congregation	180	170	450	460
Sunday Scholars	120	120	120	120
Total	300	290	570	580

A comprehensive report[14] and analysis of the census extending to over 400 pages was submitted to Parliament in 1853 but interpretation of the data should be approached with caution. Some returns were over optimistic with regard to the number of attendances on the appointed day and allegations were made that some places of worship arranged for the congregations to be 'packed'. In addition the survey recorded attendances only so that a parishioner present at both the morning and afternoon services at St Peter's Church was counted twice. A further complication arises because the report consolidated the attendances so that it was not possible to distinguish between the congregation and Sunday school attendees which had been separately recorded in the parish returns. Also, not all forms were returned and some responses were declared *'defective'* with the attendance rate estimated for the purposes of the report.

The attendances recorded at national, county and local levels taken from the report and local returns were:

Religious Survey 1851- Attendances (Church of England)				
Population	Morning	Afternoon	Evening	Total
England & Wales 17,927,609	2,371,732	1,764,641	803,141	4,939,514
Hertfordshire 167,298	32,799	32,689	5483	70,971
London Colney see below	260	570	-	830

There are problems in attempting to compare the attendance rate at St Peter's Church, London Colney, with the national and county results not only as a result of the matters discussed above but also the difficulty in precisely identifying the potential congregation within the several enumeration districts of the 1851 population census which encompassed the ecclesiastical district of the church. Nevertheless, the indications are that the rate of attendance at St Peter's Church was not less than the average and may have been considerably better.

Erskine May, in his Constitutional History[15], summarised the findings of the survey;

> For the population of England and Wales, amounting in 1851 to 17,927,609, there were 34,467 places of worship, of which 14,077 belonged to the Church of England. Accommodation was provided for 9,467,738 persons, of whom 4,922,412 were in the establishment [Church of England]. On the 30th of March, 4,428,338 attended morning service, of whom 2,371,732 were members of the church. Hence it has been computed that there were 7,646,948 members of the establishment habitually attending religious worship; and 4,466,266 nominal members rarely, if ever, attending the services of their church. These two classes united, formed about 67 per cent. of the population. The same computation reckoned 2,264,324 Wesleyans, and 610,786 Roman Catholics. The clergy of the established church numbered 17,320: ministers of other communions, 6,405.

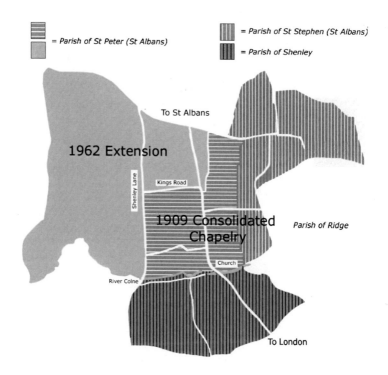

The 4 parishes converging at London Colney
Boundaries of 1909 Consolidated Chapelry and 1962 extension

In an echo of the concern expressed today with regard to church attendance, Horace Mann, the compiler of the parliamentary report commented that '*it must be apparent that a sadly formidable portion of the English people are habitual neglecters of the public ordinances of religion*' in particular '*the labouring myriads*' who '*fill, perhaps, in youth, our national, British, and Sunday Schools, and there receive the elements of a religious education; but, no sooner do they mingle in the active world of labour than, subjected to the constant action of opposing influences, they soon become as utter strangers to religious ordinances as the people of a heathen company*'

Perpetual Curates were licensed and, unlike vicars, did not undergo institution and induction to a benefice but over the years the differences between perpetual curates/vicars and chapelries/parishes became so blurred as to be indistinguishable for all practical purposes. The distinction between perpetual curates and vicars was lessened by the Clerical Subscription Act of 1865 under which both made the same oaths and declarations; and, again, in 1868 following the Incumbents Act of that year which enabled perpetual curates to adopt the courtesy title of vicar. As payment of ecclesiastical income became more centralised the distinction became even less apparent. A significant event in the history of St Peter's Church, London Colney, occurred in 1909 with the creation of the *'The Consolidated Chapelry of St Peter, Colney'* by the Order of the Ecclesiastical Commissioners[16]:

> Whereas at certain extremities of the said parish of Saint Peter (Saint Albans), of the parish of Saint Stephen (Saint Albans), and of the parish of Shenley, both in the said county and diocese, which said extremities lie contiguous one to another......there is collected together a population which is situate at a distance from the several churches of such parishes.
>
> And whereas it appears to us to be expedient that certain contiguous portions (being the portions containing the population aforesaid) of the said parish of Saint Peter (Saint Albans), of the said parish of Saint Stephen (Saint Albans), and of the said parish of Shenley should be formed into a consolidated chapelry for all ecclesiastical purposes, and that the same should be assigned to the said church of Saint Peter, Colney, situate as aforesaid.

The status of St Peter's Church, London Colney, was thus further enhanced and regarded as a separate and distinct parish by clergy and laity alike. On 1 November 2009 a celebratory service conducted by the Right Reverend Christopher Foster, Bishop of Hertford, was held to commemorate the centenary of this important landmark in the history of the church. In the strictest of terms, however, chapelries and perpetual curacies were not abolished until a Pastoral Measure of 1968.

The alterations to the boundaries in 1909 omitted the section of Ridge parish which was then within the parish of St Marks, Colney Heath, that had been established in 1845. There were further amendments in 1962[17] when the boundary was extended northwards from Kings Road to the North Orbital Road (now the A 414) and westwards to include the site of Napsbury Hospital which has since been developed with housing. The future of St Peter's Church came under scrutiny in 1998 when Michael Beer relinquished his incumbency and consideration was given to amalgamation with neighbouring parishes administered by a team ministry. The Reverend Hilary Derham was appointed as priest-in-charge holding the ministry under licence whilst the deliberations of the diocese continued. However, following her retirement in 2003 the decision was taken to permit the parish of St Peter's Church, London Colney, to maintain its independent status.

There were also changes to the patronage which together with the Tyttenhanger estate had passed to Catherine (1786-1863), daughter of the 3rd Earl of Hardwicke, who had married the 2nd Earl of Caledon. By the end of the 19th century the patron was the Dowager Countess, Elizabeth (1857-1939), widow of the 4th Earl of Caledon, and in 1910 patronage was transferred to a board of trustees:

Trustees of Patronage 1910	
Lady Elizabeth (1857-1939)	Dowager Countess of Caledon
Honourable Walter Alexander (1849-1934)	2nd son of James, 3rd Earl of Caledon
Right Honourable James Grimston (1852-1924)	3rd Earl of Verulam
Reverend Robert Squires	Vicar of St Peter's Church (St Albans)
Reverend Donald Gotto	Vicar of Shenley

Provision was made for the appointment of replacement trustees as the need arose but in May 1980 an Order was promulgated 'effecting the transfer of the ownership of the advowsons of the benefices of St Peter, Colney; and Ridge in the diocese of Saint Albans' to the Bishop of St Albans 'in his corporate capacity'[18] and patronage is presently governed by the Patronage (Benefices) Measure of 1986.

---

[1] *Quarterly Theological Review 1826* C & J Rivington Volume III p 529
[2] www.theclergydatabase.org.uk citing reference Guildhall Library 9532/a/2 (Episcopal Act Book)
[3] CERC: correspondence 7 April 1826 FP Howley 31 f 432-44v
[4] ibid
[5]*County Chronicle* 25 July 1826 p 2
[6] LPL: Correspondence 15 July 1826 ICBS 00463
[7] LPL: Letter FP Blomfield 71f 31r
[8] LPL: Articles of Enquiry FP Blomfield 71 f 33r
[9] LPL: Rural Dean's Return FP Blomfield 72 f 169v
[10] HALS: Licences for marriages to be solemnised DP93B/2/1

[11] HALS: ibid
[12] HALS: ibid
[13] Alasdair Crockett *Variations in Churchgoing Rates in England in 1851,* University of Oxford Discussion Paper in Economic and Social History No 36 August 2000
[14] Census of Great Britain, 1851, Religious Worship, England & Wales, Report & Tables HMSO 1853
[15] Sir Thomas Erskine May *The Constitutional History of England since George The Third 1760-1860* (7th Edition Vol 3 1882) pp 233-234
[16] HALS: DS1/3/3/3
[17] HALS: DS1/3/3/8
[18] HALS: DS1/3/3/12

CHAPTER FOUR

The Church Building

St Peter's Church, London Colney, is of a plain yet pleasing design that creates an ambience of intimacy for the worshippers. An early example of the Norman Revival style of architecture, and now designated a Grade II listed building, the church is located within the London Colney Conservation Area that was created in 1974 under the provisions of the Civic Amenities Act of 1967. Funded with the aid of a grant from the Church Building Society, the design of St Peter's Church was influenced by the rules of the Society stipulating that '...*no expense shall be incurred for ornamental architecture beyond what shall...be deemed essential to give the buildings...the character of Churches or Chapels of the Church of England [Rule 20]*'[1].

The church lies on a north-west and south-east alignment rather that the more traditional east-west ecclesiastical compass (*ec*). The south-east façade (*ec* west), originally rendered in stucco, incorporates a flight of steps providing access to the ribbed main access doors set in a doorway formed with a double set of shafts on either side having scalloped capitals above and narrower blind arches on either side supporting the doorway itself. There are further blind arches at ground floor level with decorative mouldings below the upper side windows. Above the entrance, echoing the lines of the doorway, there is a three light window with round-headed arches and shafts with scalloped capitals on the mullions and jambs all in stucco. Two single light windows flank the main window again with stucco semi-circular heads and mouldings with a stone cross on the ridge of the roof. With the exception of the uppermost section of the middle light of the centre window, all of the glazed lights at this level are screened internally with a barrier of brick and plaster. It remains a matter of speculation whether the obstruction of the windows was an original feature of the chapel or introduced at a later date.

Four 2-stage brick buttresses support the façade; the inner buttresses, and repeated on the north-west (*ec* east) elevation, originally incorporated a third upper stage surmounted by a spire pinnacle which have been successively removed. Within the apex of the roof there is a protruding louvred chamber for the wheel

London Colney History Society

1906 looking across River Colne towards St Peter's Church

mounted bell which was cast at the Mears foundry in Whitechapel at a cost of £16-16s-0d (£16.80)[2]. Donated by the promoter of the chapel, the bell bears the inscription '*The gift of Thomas Newcome Rector of Shenley 1825*'. His diary records a visit to the foundry made in October 1825 and his presence when the bell was hung later the same month. The buttresses are repeated on the north-west (*ec* east) elevation and an early print of the church depicts a weather vane surmounting the roof. Each of the flank walls of soft red brick incorporates a series of single light windows set in cast iron grid framings, having radial fins at each semi-circular head, holding rectangular glazed panes, together with a series of composite buttresses.

The interior of the chapel was constructed simply with plastered walls and flooring of flagstones and terra cotta tiles. The sanctuary recess and altar were located at the north-west (*ec* east) end of the church with a nearby doorway providing access to a small vestry. Within the void above the barrel vaulted roof there are various features of the timberwork suggesting that that the original roof structure was not sound and that an additional set of rafters was installed[3].

The capacity of the church was also dictated by the rules of the Church Building Society which stipulated that its initial grant of £400 was subject to the provision of 750 sittings. In order to accommodate the congregation, galleries, supported on cast iron pillars, were installed along the south-west (*ec* north), north-east (*ec* south) and south-east (*ec* west) walls with two access staircases abutting the south-east wall (*ec* west). Following the consecration of the chapel in July 1826, a certificate[4] was issued confirming the seating arrangements:

> The Undersigned hereby Certify that the Chapel of Saint Peter London Colney in the County of Hertford has been Erected and finished under his superintenance and direction, and is now Completed; that the said Chapel containing sittings for 750 Persons 375 of which are Free.
> The Free Seats are located as follows
> All the Seats (being five rows in number) under the end or front Gallery
> The whole of the Gallery (except the Pews at the North Eastern and North Western ends thereof containing a length of 13 feet from the end wall on the North Eastern, and 9 feet on the North Western ends – by the width of the Gallery) that is from the side Walls of the Chapel to the Gallery fronts respectively.
> George Smith
> Architect
> Mercers Hall
> London
> 15 September 1826
> Markland Barnard BA Trinty College Cambridge
> Minister of St Peter Colney Chapel
> John Jaques Chapel Warden
> Thomas Barnett Chapel Warden

The return made for the purposes of the 1851 Ecclesiastical Census confirms the number of sittings at 750 and the Post Office Directory of Hertfordshire and Middlesex published in 1855 describes the chapel at London Colney as '...*a neat square building, with double aisle and galleries and capable of containing 750 persons*'. The timber flooring beneath the present arrangement of pews (2009) has inserts corresponding with distance between the inner pillars of the remaining south-east (*ec* west) gallery indicating the position of the 2 aisles. With overhanging galleries to 3 sides of the church blocking natural light and tightly packed rows of pews

Hertfordshire Archives and Local Studies

Circa 1840 St Peter's Church, London Colney
Note spire pinnacles and weather vane

E A Sweetman & Son Ltd

Circa 1930 St Peter's Church, London Colney
Note spire pinnacles

John Webb

1983 St Peter's Church, London Colney
Note spire pinnacles removed

John Webb

1996 St Peter's Church, London Colney
Note Upper buttresses removed

across the body of the nave, there was little to relieve the stark appearance of the building but after the passage of some 40 years significant improvements were made.

In 1865 members of the Caledon and Hardwicke families, patrons and benefactors of St Peter's Church, donated the impressive stained glass window which dominates the church today (see front cover). A nearby brass plate (which no longer exists), described in the centenary booklet, was inscribed as follows:

> This Window is placed by Elizabeth, Baroness Stuart de Rothsay, Jane Countess of Caledon, and her son James 4th Earl of Caledon, in memory of Philip 3rd Earl of Hardwicke and Elizabeth Countess of Hardwicke, of Dupre 2nd Earl of Caledon, and Catherine Freman Countess of Caledon, the founders and benefactors of this church. A.D. 1865

According to the booklet the window was designed by Louisa, Dowager Marchioness of Waterford, granddaughter of Philip, 3rd Earl of Hardwicke, a noted watercolourist of her time, several of whose works are held in the National Portrait Gallery collection.

The 3 light window depicts the suspended figure of Christ ascending into Heaven attended by 2 angels under the marvelling gaze of the Apostles. Each of the lights contains part of the figurative scene with upper and lower decorative panels; the lower panels carry biblical texts. It is likely that in her design the Marchioness of Waterford was influenced by classical interpretations of the Ascension such as the 'Transfiguration' by Raphael (1517-1520).

Text Panels		
Location	Text	Source
Banner	Why stand ye gazing up into Heaven this same Jesus which is taken up from you into Heaven shall so come in like manner as ye have seen him go into Heaven	Acts Ch 1 v 11
South-west light	Blessed are the dead which die in the Lord even so saith the spirit for they rest from their labours and their works do follow them	Revelation Ch 14 v 13

Centre light	I will ransom them from the power of the grave I will redeem them from death O death I will be thy plagues O grave I will be thy destruction	Hosea Ch 13 v 14
North-east light	I am the resurrection & the life saith the Lord he that believeth in me though he were dead yet shall he live & whosoever liveth & believeth in me shall never die	John Ch 11 v 25-26

The window bears the maker's name 'Hughes London 1865'. Henry Hughes (1822-1883), in partnership with Thomas Ward (1808-1870), was a leading maker of stained glass windows in the mid 19th century employing over 100 staff at times of peak production; trading as Ward & Hughes the window is unusual for being 'signed' solely by Hughes. Before manufacture, and using a water colour sketch provided by the Marchioness, the glass maker would have created a full size drawing of the window indicating the position of the supporting glazing bars (ferramenta) and the lead lines holding each glass piece. Typically, the design of the surrounding panels was left to the discretion of the maker and the lower panels of the Ascension window bearing the texts are decorated with oak leaves and acorns.

That same year (1865) a pipe organ was built and installed at a cost of £155 by Hill & Son to the order of Reverend Markland Barnard. William Hill (1789-1870) is considered by many to be the finest 19th century builder of British organs and, in 1861, had been responsible for the organ installed at St Albans Abbey for the more substantial sum of £1,100. As the organ was contemporaneous with the installation of the Ascension window, it can be speculated that the Caledon family also contributed towards the cost. A reference in the Centenary booklet suggests that an earlier organ, likely to have been a simpler instrument, was located in the gallery.

The organ at St Peter's has a single manual (keyboard) with 10 stops controlling nine ranks of pipes, 444 pipes in total. Built before the position of the pedals was standardised, the straight, short compass, pedalboard is offset to the manual keyboard thus presenting a challenge for present day organists. Until the introduction of electricity to the church in 1947 the organ bellows were operated manually. Over the years, the decoration on the

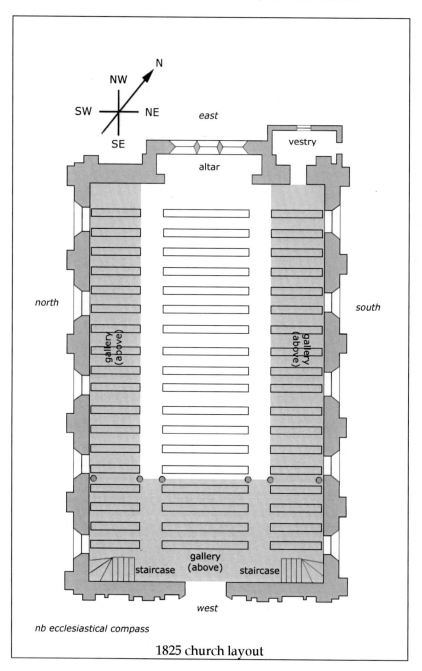

nb ecclesiastical compass

1825 church layout

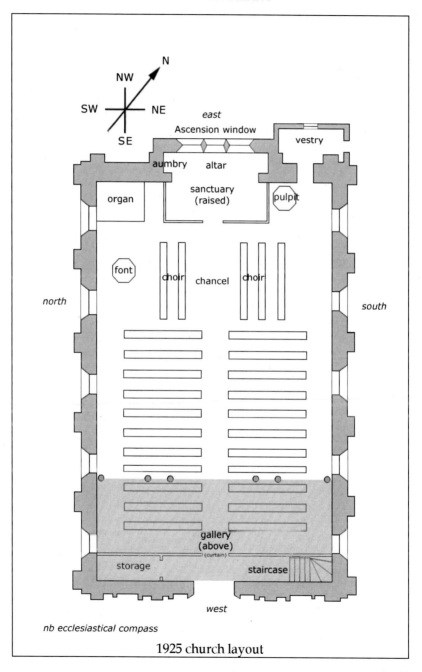

N
NW
SW · NE
SE

east
Ascension window

vestry

aumbry altar

organ

sanctuary
(raised)

pulpit

font

choir chancel choir

north

south

gallery
(above)

(curtain)

storage

staircase

west

nb ecclesiastical compass

1925 church layout

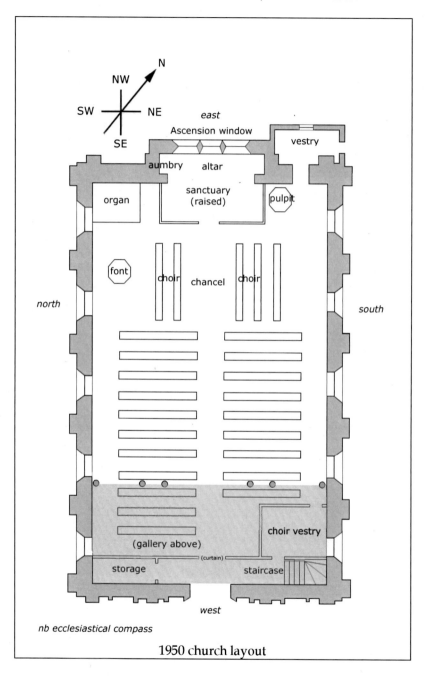

1950 church layout

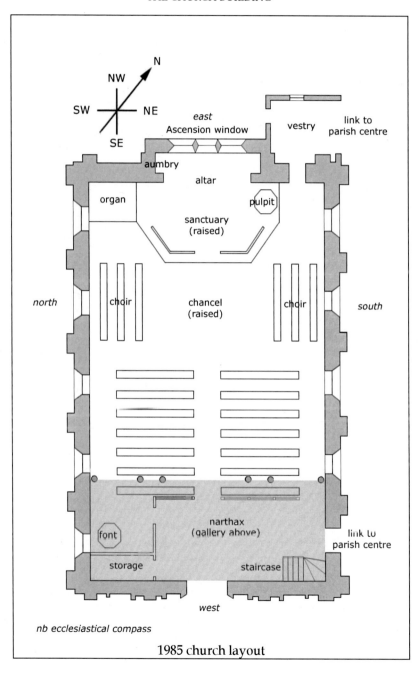

N

NW

SW —|— NE

SE

east
Ascension window

vestry

link to
parish centre

aumbry

altar

organ

pulpit

sanctuary
(raised)

north

choir

chancel
(raised)

choir

south

narthax
(gallery above)

font

link to
parish centre

storage

staircase

west

nb ecclesiastical compass

1985 church layout

organ pipes believed to have been painted by the son of the first minister, Reverend Markland Barnard (1825-1892), deteriorated and was restored by a later churchwarden, Herbert Beadle.

2009 William Hill organ

In 1991 the organ was carefully restored by Hill, Norman & Beard, successors of William Hill. On dismantling, it was discovered that the floor beneath the instrument had rotted and partially collapsed causing distortion of the soundboard. Works to repair the flooring and restore the organ were estimated at some £14,000 and caused consideration to be given to using the organ casing to house an electronic instrument. Fortunately a grant of £11,000 was obtained which enabled the work to proceed. The restoration was non-invasive and the organ is now considered to be a fine and historically important example of a William Hill instrument retaining almost all of the original pipework [Appendix 4]. Of particular note is the Cornopean, a stop invented by William Hill, which retains its original brass tongues.

Steps were taken in 2002 to bring the instrument to the attention of the British Institute of Organ Studies, a society dedicated to the promotion, conservation and preservation of historic organs which are *often neglected and misunderstood having a relatively low priority in terms of restoration and conservation for hard pressed PCCs and congregations'*. After an inspection the organ at St Peter's was awarded a Grade II* [Grade 2 star] Historic Organ Certificate in 2003 *'being a good example of Hill c1865 substantially unaltered'*, the only graded organ in Hertfordshire listed on the National Pipe Organ Register. In recent years musical accompaniment was supplemented by an upright piano that was replaced by a Clavinova electronic instrument in 2002 and the piano moved to the parish centre.

The concomitant installation of the Ascension window and Hill organ in 1865 suggests that the work was possibly part of greater re-ordering of the church which included the dismantling of the side galleries (with a consequent reduction in the number of sittings), removal of one of the access staircases, re-arrangement of the pews creating a central and 2 side aisles, and the installation of the 4 decorative (non-load bearing) roof trusses that span the ceiling. Later trade directories describe the church as *'a plain rectangular brick building, with a gallery at the west [ecclesiastical compass] end [and] will seat 600 persons'*[5].

A further re-ordering mentioned in the centenary booklet was undertaken in the early 20th century:

> About twenty years ago [circa 1905], however, the church was reseated, so that there are not now sittings for so many. At this time the present choir stalls were introduced, and arranged facing one another, and the pews behind were also placed sideways to the altar. Before this time all the pews faced the altar, and they were more closely packed together...At the same time the walls were painted as they are now. Before this time the choir had been in the gallery

Throughout the first half of the 20th century alterations to the lay-out of the church continued to be made. A screen separating the chancel from the nave was erected in 1930 and removed in 1945 during the ministry of Thomas Barber. Spanning the width of the church the screen was decorated with *'barley sugar columns'* and incorporated a large archway over the centre aisle with a smaller archway on either side[6]. A Children's Corner was created in 1934 in front of the organ and furnished with *'a small Holy Table, two Candlesticks and a Crucifix, a picture of "The Madonna and Child" and three plaster figures'*; and in 1951 a choir vestry was constructed by screening off the eastern corner (*ec* south-west) of the church beneath the remaining gallery.

Oil lamps and candles had provided illumination until gas lighting was installed in 1911 which, in turn, was replaced by electricity in 1947. Fund raising to install an electricity supply to the church had been commenced 10 years earlier in 1937 but, no doubt, was interrupted by the outbreak of World War 2. The 1947 installation comprised a series of wall mounted lights along each side wall and the chancel recess together with ceiling lights under the balcony. At the time of this work the opportunity was taken to remove the coal slow burning 'Tortoise' stove, which had become a favoured source of heating for churches after its introduction in 1830, and replaced with gas heating. The stove was positioned against the north-east (*ec* south) wall of the church and the external brick flue remains in situ. The gas heating system was renewed in 1990 and again in 2009.

In 1970 the wall mounted brackets were disconnected and lighting was provided by suspended multi-light pendants. In 1980 the church was completely rewired replacing the rubber insulated wire and in 2000, following suitable trials, the design and installation of the present lighting system of down lighters and spot lights (2009) was undertaken by 2 church volunteers. A sound system was installed in 1989 and enhanced 4 years later together with the introduction of an induction loop for the hard of hearing. Further improvements to the sound equipment were made in 2004, in part to cater for the requirements of the youth musical group, 'Resurrection', which was particularly active at that time.

A major re-ordering of the church took place in 1980 when, after deliberation and consultation, a decision was taken to:

> raise the sanctuary in order improve sight lines and audibility
> provide improved access around the altar and communion rails

provide a more flexible are for special events such as drama
presentations and concerts
completely re-decorate the church interior
lay carpeting in the church
re-position and lower the pulpit

In order to achieve these aims raised flooring was installed in
the chancel and sanctuary. The choir stalls were moved further
apart and the book rests adapted to be removable; the altar was
moved forward into the sanctuary; the altar rails were modified
and re-positioned; and the pulpit was modified and re-sited.
Hardworking and enthusiastic volunteers, including the minister,
Michael Beer, carried out the work over several weeks. In March
1983 a faculty was obtained for the installation of an aumbrey (or
sacrament safe) within the wall of the sanctuary to enable the
consecrated elements from the communion service to be retained
and taken to the sick unable to attend church. The aumbrey is
furnished with an oak surround and door carved by Len Laidlaw,
a parishioner.

Structural alterations were necessary to the building in 1985 in
order to accommodate a link with the newly constructed parish
centre. The solution adopted was to break through the window
opening at the south-east end of the north-eastern (ec south) wall of
the church in order to insert a doorway. Internally, the timber
screen in front of the entrance was removed together with the
small choir vestry that had been added in 1951. In its place a
glazed screen was erected beneath the gallery spanning over half
the width of the church and creating a narthex (entrance lobby).
Refurbishment of the entrance doors was undertaken and a small
plaque on the interior of the doors commemorates William
Sammels who died, aged 74, in 1987. Associated with the
construction of the parish centre the small vestry at the north-west
(ec east) end of the church was demolished and a considerably
enlarged room that connected with the centre was built. Externally,
by 1989, the rendering on the facade of the church was loosing
adhesion and was removed exposing the substrate brickwork. The
fabric was found to be in good order and a decision was taken to
re-point and leave the brickwork exposed thus blending well with
the recently built parish centre.

End notes

[1] *The Christian Journal and Literary Register 1818* p 158

[2] *County Herald* 24 December 1825

[3] CA: Peter Dalling & Associates *Quinquennial Inspection Report* p 14

[4] LPL: Correspondence ICBS 00463

[5] *Kelly's Directory for Hertfordshire* 1882

[6] Margaret Hopkins

CHAPTER FIVE

Furnishings, Plate, Memorials and Charities

Internally the original furnishings of the chapel echoed the simplicity of the architectural design although the austere surroundings were relieved partially by 2 metal boards decorated with illuminated script, one of which recited the 10 commandments whilst the other repeated the Lords Prayer and the Creed. At the time of the consecration in 1826 it was the responsibility of churchwardens to ensure that the 10 Commandments and other selected sacred texts were displayed[1]. Until 1925 the boards remained in position on either side of the altar but later were relocated to the south-east (*ec* west) wall behind the gallery.

Tightly packed rows of pews filled the body of the church but in 1905, as described in the centenary booklet, '*The old pews were removed, and the present seats put in their place. They are much more comfortable*' and choir stalls placed sideways to the altar were installed. A major reordering of the church in 1980 resulted in additional pews, taken from the gallery, being positioned adjacent to the choir stalls. Chairs were substituted in the gallery for the repositioned pews and, in turn, were replaced in 2005 by 7 pews acquired from the former chapel of Napsbury Hospital, which had become part of the Arboretum housing development.

During the early years of the church, the vessel used for baptisms may have been a simple utensil because, although the first baptism at the chapel was performed shortly after consecration, nevertheless, in his diary entry of 17 March 1842, Thomas Newcome, the promoter of the new chapel and rector of Shenley, commented that he '*...gave a font to Colney Chapel*'. Thus the comment in the centenary booklet that the font '*is of exactly the same design as that at Shenley Parish Church*' is explained. Over the years the font has been variously located within the church. In the 1980 re-ordering it was positioned at the south-east (*ec* west) end although a portable font was utilised for baptisms until it was replaced with an improved font in 1992 comprising a shallow vessel supported on an oak cruciform stand.

John Webb

2010 Arrangement of pews

Ken Barker

Pulpit

Ken Barker

Font

A wooden pulpit, decorated with floral carvings, and a lectern completed the furnishings. The centenary booklet also explains that an existing lectern was replaced with a brass lectern donated by Andrew Trollope who was headmaster of the nearby Tyttenhanger Lodge preparatory school during the later 19th and early 20th centuries and sometime churchwarden. In 1982, Michael Beer, minister 1980-1987, carved a figure of the Risen and Ascended Christ for display at Verulam House, the former diocesan retreat and conference centre in St Albans, which was brought to St Peter's Church in 1994 upon closure of the retreat and in 2010 adorns the gallery balustrade. In recent years there have been several presentations of church furniture dedicated to the memory of parishioners and others; 1977 a pair of small prayer desks (prideau) in memory of Joan Roberts nee Booty, sister of John Booty, minister 1949-1979; 1994 glazed oak display cabinet for the memorial book in memory of George Scott; 1995 votive candle stand in memory of Peter Ridout; 1997 oak lectern in memory of Julie Emerick.

Flagon donated by
Earl of Hardwicke

In addition to providing land for the church and contributing towards the building costs, Philip, 3rd Earl of Hardwicke, donated the church plate too comprising a cup (chalice); paten (plate for Eucharistic bread); a communion flagon inscribed *'The Gift of the Right Hon. The Earl of Hardwicke to London Colney Chapel 1825'*; and an alms dish. With the exception of the alms dish, each item bore the maker's mark (a hand) of Nathaniel Smith of Sheffield. The flagon and alms dish survive and continue in use. There have been additions to, and disposals of, the church plate and altar furniture over the history of the church. The additions include; circa 1917 silver cross *'In honour of*

51

1925 Note:
text boards either
side of altar,
brass lectern,
gas lighting.

R O Sanders

the most Holy Sacrament of the Altar and in loving memory of his servant Donald Gotto Priest' Rector of Shenley, a successor of Thomas Newcome and one of the patronage trustees of St Peter's Church, London Colney, appointed in 1910; 1927 a ciborium dedicated to the memory of Lina Mary Richardson; 1929 chalice and paten donated by the Confraternity of the Blessed Sacrament, an anglo-catholic organisation, during the incumbency of Thomas Barber; 1965 gold painted cross in memory of Tom Bontoft; 1985 wafer box in memory of Elsie Jackson.

Three memorials are set in the chancel floor commemorating parishioners whose earthly remains are interred in brick vaults beneath. Their location does not correspond with the vaults and, if in their present position when the early layout of the church incorporated 2 aisles, the memorials would have been covered with pews. It is likely, therefore, that the tablets were relocated and possibly during the re-ordering of the church in 1865. The memorials remained exposed, until covered by the raised flooring installed at the time of the 1980 church re-ordering, and each is

John Webb

1980 After re-ordering

badly worn by the passage of countless worshippers. The earliest memorial is dedicated to William Pryor who died on 17 January 1828, aged 78, and whose interment was the first burial at St Peter's Church.

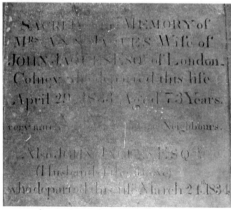

Memorial to John and Ann Jaques

A second is inscribed to the memory of Ann Jaques, wife of the 1st churchwarden, who died in May 1833 aged 73 and her husband, John, who passed away 11 months later in April 1834 at the age of 82. Lettering of the third memorial has been almost obliterated but there is sufficient information to identify the burial records for William Joseline, aged 84, in March 1842 and his wife, Lydia, who predeceased him in January 1841.

Two memorial tablets adorn the north-east wall (*ec* south) of the church. Firstly:

Near this tablet lies all that was mortal of
MARY,
The beloved, beloving, and devoted wife of
William Swainson, F.R.S., etc.,
The tender mother of five children, from whom her Lord
And saviour took her on 12th of Feb., 1835.
Blessed are the pure in heart, for they shall see God. – Matth. V. 8.
She is not dead – but sleepeth. – Luke viii. 52.

William Swainson
(1789-1855)

William Swainson (1789-1855) was an eminent naturalist who lived at Highfield Hall in Tyttenhanger. He was elected Fellow of the Royal Society in 1820 and after the death of his wife in 1835 he emigrated to New Zealand in 1840 where he died in 1855 aged 66. Thomas Newcome, Rector of Shenley, was a friend of William Swainson and godfather to his son Edwin Swainson[2]. The two men often dined together and continued to correspond after the emigration.

The second, much later, tablet, commemorates Florence Barber who died on Boxing Day 1943. Florence was the first wife of Thomas Barber, the incumbent of St Peter's Church from 1928 until 1948:

In Loving memory of
Florence Guy Barber
wife of the Vicar of this Parish
and President of
the Womens Section,
British Legion London Colney Branch
This tablet is erected by the members
in recognition of her work
1933-1943.

Florence was also a staunch supporter of the Mothers' Union whose members presented an inscribed processional cross to the church in her memory.

Three inscriptions previously displayed in the church and mentioned in the centenary booklet have not survived. One of them, a brass plate beneath the Ascension window (see chapter 4), was also described in an earlier publication[3] :

> This window is placed by Elizabeth, Baroness Stuart de Rothsay, Jane Countess of Caledon, and her son James 4th Earl of Caledon, in memory of Philip 3rd Earl of Hardwicke and Elizabeth Countess of Hardwicke, of Dupre 2nd Earl of Caledon, and Catherine Freman Countess of Caledon, the founders and benefactors of this church. A.D. 1865.

Two further inscriptions were located beneath the gallery, the first providing details of the reduced number of sittings following the removal of the side galleries:

> This church was erected in the year 1825; it contains sittings for 600 persons, and in consequence of a grant from the Society for Promoting the Enlargement and Building of Churches and Chapels, 375 sittings are hereby declared to be free and unappropriated for ever.
> The Rev. Markland Barnard, M.A., Minister.
> John Jaques, Esq.,
> Mr. Thomas Barnet, Churchwardens

The second inscription beneath the gallery, according to the centenary booklet, was '...*not easy to read as it has been partially effaced by the damp*' and recorded one of the 3 charities associated with the church. Commonly known as the 'bread charity' the fund had been bestowed by the will of the first churchwarden, John Jaques, who died in 1833:

> John Jaques, Esq., bequeathed the interest of 200 3 per cent. Consols [Government stocks] to be laid out in the purchase of bread, and distributed according to the discretion of the minister of Colney, among poor people residing at London Colney, and in the neighbourhood of that place, exclusively to widows and labouring men with families. Such distribution to be made in equal proportions on the last day of February and on the 9th day of November in each year.

A secondary source[4] mentions that the proceeds of the charity were intended for families living in that part of London Colney which was situated within the civil parish of St Peter (St Albans).

A second charity ('the blanket charity') arose from the proximity of the church to Colney House, a substantial country house that stood on the site of All Saints Pastoral Centre in Shenley Lane. From 1832 until 1871 the house was in the possession of the Oddie family. Henry Hoyle Oddie, a wealthy solicitor, died in 1847 leaving his widow, Georgiana (1795-1862), in occupation of the property. In 1850, the youngest daughter, Ellen Oddie, married the Reverend James Lewis Walker Venables who died 2 years later and bequeathed £100 in his will to his mother-in-law 'so as to enable her to add to the benefits she confers annually on the poor in the place where she now lives'[5]. The legacy was invested £98 4s 6d 3% Consols and the dividends used to distribute blankets at Christmas time to the deserving poor with preference being given to those '...of that part of Colney St Peter which lies in the ancient parish of Shenley'[6]. By 1887 the distribution of the charity was at the discretion of the incumbent of St Peter's Church, London Colney[7].

The third charity ('coal charity') was the bequest of Charles Morris (1865-1826) a successful engineer and businessman who moved into Highfield Hall, Tyttenhanger, and became a benefactor of good causes in London Colney and Colney Heath. His will left the sum of £250 to the 'Vicar and churchwardens for the time being of the Parish of London Colney' for the establishment of a charitable trust with the income thereof distributed 'amongst such poor inhabitants of the Parish ...as they shall think deserving for the purpose of enabling such persons to buy warm clothing and fuel'. In 1930 the legacy was invested in the purchase of £257 5s 7d 5% War Stock.

By the time of the ministries of John Booty and Michael Beer distribution of the 'bread charity' was implemented with vouchers that could be redeemed at the small grocer's shop opposite the vicarage in the slip road providing access to Waterside and the Green Dragon Inn. Income from the 'blanket' and 'coal' charities had been merged and used to contribute towards the fuel bills of needy families. Inflation and social change, however, had rendered the charities, with a total annual income of less than £25, obsolete. The position of such small charities, repeated countless times nationally, was addressed by the Charities Act of 1985 which enabled the original objectives of a charity to be modified. At St Peter's Church, London Colney, advantage of the Act was taken to wind up the charities and realise the assets which were allocated to upkeep of the church fabric.

Two of the several charities, some dating from the 16th century, associated with the former mother church of St Peter's, St Albans, had connections with London Colney. A series of statutes between 1853-1869 made provision for the better administration of charitable trusts and in 1881, by an agreement with the Charity Commissioners, these several charities were amalgamated into the 'Church Lands' and the 'Church and Poor Lands' charities jointly administered by a board of local trustees[8]. Amongst the properties comprising the Church Lands Charity were *'Two Cottages at London Colney, adjoining the "Chequers Inn", now let at rents amounting together to £10 8s [£10.40] per annum'*[9] and which were sold in 1922 with the proceeds invested in Government Stocks. The income from the charity did not, however, benefit the parishioners of London Colney, and was applied *'...primarily in defraying any charges lawfully incurred...in the maintenance and repair of the fabric of the Parish Church of St. Peter, St. Albans'*[10].

Financial advantage did accrue from the Church and Poor Lands Charity the net income of which, by the terms of the 1881 agreement, was *'...for the benefit of deserving and necessitous persons, being bona fide resident inhabitants of the...Parish of St Peter, St Albans, to be selected...by the Trustees'*[11]. By a further scheme of 1910 the specified needs of St Peter's, St Albans, were made first charge on the income of the charity but, from any surplus, up to £150 each could be paid its *'daughter churches'*. Allocation of the surplus income was agreed at the annual meetings of the trustees and in 1903 the distribution to London Colney amounted to £5[12] increasing to £34[13] by 1970. This arrangement came to an end in 1995 when daughter churches were removed from the qualifying beneficiaries and the current recipients are the St Albans Churches of St Peter's, St Paul's and St Luke's.

End notes
[1] Sir Thomas Edlyne Tomlins *The Law Dictionary* 1835
[2] Knight, Judith & Flood, Susan *Two Nineteenth century Hertfordshire Diaries 1822-1849* (Hertfordshire Record Society 2002) ISBN 0952377977 pp 126 & 183n
[3] *History of Hertfordshire* – Vol 3 Cassio Hundred 1881 John Cussans p 39
[4] ibid p40

[5] *History of the County of Hertford* Victoria County History 1908 Vol 2
[6] ibid
[7] HALS: Terrier 1887 DP93B-3-8
[8] HALS: 1881 Scheme DP93/25/4
[9] HALS: List of Charities DP93/25/17
[10] HALS: supra no 8
[11] HALS: supra no 8
[12] HALS: Distribution DP/93/25/20
[13] HALS: Distribution DP/93/25/23

CHAPTER SIX

The Churchyard

A t the time the London Colney chapel was built draconian punishments under ecclesiastical law passed in the reign of Elizabeth I remained available for misbehaviour in churchyards and '...*striking with a weapon, or drawing with such intent in any church-yard, is punishable with loss of ears, burning [branding] and excommunication*'[1]. Approximately ¼ acre of the land provided by Phillip, 3rd Earl of Hardwicke, for the new chapel at London Colney was set aside as the burial ground although, on financial grounds, Thomas Newcome, the promoter, expressed the opinion that '...*the Chapel yard behind the Chapel would be more use to the Minister as a Garden Again than as a Burial Ground and sale of it would diminish the debt*'[2].

By the end of the 19th century additional land for burials was becoming a matter for concern. The north-west extremity of the churchyard abutted a paddock in the demise of a nearby house in the High Street, Colney Villa, that had been inherited by Mary Summers on the death of her mother, Jane, in 1892. In 1903 Mary Summers agreed with the vicar, Thomas Bluett, to sell a ¼ acre (1210 square yards) of the paddock for £125 and the land was conveyed to the Ecclesiastical Commissioners[3] on 3 August 1903. After the newly acquired land had been prepared a Petition[4] was submitted to the Bishop of St Albans inviting him to consecrate the ground for burial purposes. Attested by the Vicar (Thomas Bluett), the Churchwardens (Andrew Trollope, headmaster of Tyttenhanger Lodge School, and Edwin Parsons, baker and sub-postmaster), together with 5 inhabitants of London Colney (including John Birch, the local schoolmaster and George Burr, undertaker) the Petition confirmed that '...*the portion of the said piece of land......has been properly levelled and enclosed on all sides except adjoining the said Churchyard and is now in a fit and proper condition for interments and may be advantageously added to and form part of the said Churchyard*. The Bishop of St Albans, Edgar Jacob, accepted the Petition and declared the added ground consecrated on 22 May 1904[5]. Thirty years later, however, additional space was again required and in 1934, the minister, Thomas Barber, estimated that '...*there was room in the existing Churchyard for Burials for 18 months*'[6].

Thomas Barber held talks with the directors of the St Albans Sand & Gravel Co Ltd, owners of land surrounding 2 sides of the churchyard[7]. An agreement was reached that the Company would sell a ½ acre plot (1 rood, 36 poles and 158 square yards) adjoining the 1903 churchyard extension for the sum of £100 together with contribution of £3.3.0 towards their own costs which the purchasers would be obliged to pay. The arrangement provided for the land to be transferred in 2 parcels on separate dates by a payment of £50 for each parcel but the respective solicitors, subsequently instructed by each party, recommended a single conveyance in order to save on costs whilst retaining the dual handover. The vendors agreed to fill an encroaching disused gravel pit and to allow possession to be transferred before the formal conveyance of the land. Negotiations, however, between the solicitors were interrupted when it was discovered that the churchyard was subject of a Closing Order.

A Closing Order had been issued in 1856 under the Burial Act of 1853 prohibiting the opening of new burial grounds, without approval, in the civil parish of St Albans which included London Colney. It was argued unsuccessfully that the new ground was merely an addition to the 1903 extension of the churchyard which had received such approval because the Order applied not only to existing burial grounds but also extensions to them. A formal application was made to the Ministry of Health which in July 1934, after an inspection by one of its inspectors the previous month, advised that '*In view of the large open gravel pit on the site the Minister is at present unable to approve the provision and use of the whole of the site. He is, however, prepared to give his approval in respect of an area, 130 ft by 75 ft (0.224 acres)...In the alternative, he would defer his approval of the whole of the proposed site until such time as the gravel pits on the site have been completely filled in*'. The minister and his Parochial Church Council opted to accept the Ministry's first proposal and the initial payment of £50 was paid in July 1934 to St Albans Sand & Gravel Co Ltd. The conveyance of both parcels of land was completed in March 1935 and the final payment of £50 was made.

There was, however, a further obstacle to overcome following an inspection by the diocesan archdeacon in August 1935 who reported:

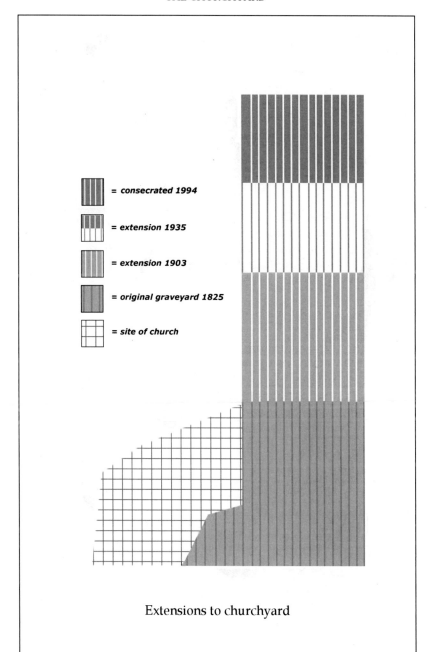

= consecrated 1994

= extension 1935

= extension 1903

= original graveyard 1825

= site of church

Extensions to churchyard

Ken Barker

2009 view of churchyard

Ken Barker

2009 Garden of Rest

> I have been asked to go and inspect a proposed addition to London Colney Churchyard with a view to consecration. I have been to see it this morning and really cannot recommend as it is at present. The whole Churchyard is disgracefully kept and the addition is covered with rough grass and weeds and the central part is overgrown. It is not properly fenced, it has a sort of privet hedge which will keep nothing out and the privet bushes are covered with weeds. I have recommended to Bishop of Bedford to postpone consecration for six months.

After a further inspection the following year the condition was considered acceptable and the parcel of land was consecrated by the Bishop of Bedford on 23 June 1936.

The comments of the archdeacon in 1935 caused the vicar and Parochial Church Council to address the maintenance of the churchyard and they came to the conclusion that was hopeless to attempt to keep it in a proper and tidy condition until the original section had been levelled wherever possible. Accordingly an application was made for permission to remove grave mounds that had been neglected and were overgrown but retaining gravestones and memorials. A faculty to proceed was granted in 1937 subject to the proviso that a scale plan should be prepared upon which the displaced mounds were to be shown. The work of clearing the churchyard was carried by volunteers from the local branch of the TOC H organisation.

The remainder of the land acquired from the St Albans Sand & Gravel Co Ltd in 1935, after it had been filled in, was not put into use until 1993. It seems that access to the conveyance evidencing the transfer of ownership was not available at that time because the current minister, Michael Beer, and his predecessor, John Booty, were obliged to provide sworn statutory declarations in order to establish a legal right of possession both of which concluded '*I am not aware of any matter or thing whereby the Incumbent of the Benefice of Colney St Peter to the said land or any part thereof may be affected questioned or doubted in any manner whatsoever*'[8]. As a further prudent measure, a policy of Defective Title Indemnity Insurance was effected with Sun Alliance & London Insurance PLC indemnifying the *The Incumbent of Colney St Peter* against disputes arising from defects with regard to the ownership or title of the land[9].

Ken Barker

2009 Headstone in 1994 Garden of Rest

By 1960 a garden of rest for cremated remains had been laid out adjacent to the south-eastern boundary of the original churchyard site and the remaining portion of the former St Albans Sand & Gravel Co Ltd land was adopted for a similar purpose. The Right Reverend Robert Runcie, formerly Archbishop of Canterbury (1980-1991) and Bishop of St Albans (1970-1979), consecrated the ground at a ceremony conducted on 15 May 1994[10]. A simple headstone declares:

REMEMBER
IN PRAYER BEFORE GOD
THOSE WHOSE ASHES
ARE INTERRED IN THIS CHURCHYARD
AND THOSE WHOSE
REMAINS REST
ELSEWHERE

Generations of London Colney families have been laid to rest in the churchyard including the first four ministers of St Peter's Church and members of their families. A memorial, comprising an obelisk mounted on a pedestal (originally enclosed within an iron railing[11]) commemorates the site of the family vault of the first incumbent, Markland Barnard, who was interred in 1895 alongside his father, Robert Barnad (1845), Jane Ireland (aunt -1845), Sophia Cope (aunt of wife - 1860) and his wife, Emma, (1893). More poignantly, until recent years, close-by there was a memorial to the infant deaths of 3 of his grandchildren. His daughter, Emma, had married Henry Yates, an officer in Royal Artillery, and in 1869 accompanied her husband to a posting on Malta. Within a period of 12 days between 27 September 1869 and 8 October 3 1869, 3 of their 6 children, Algernon, aged 2 years 10 months, Cecilia, aged 5 years 5 months, and Lionel, aged 7 years, succumbed during an outbreak of diphtheria. Successors to Markland Barnard also interred in the churchyard are; Thomas Bluett (1937) and his first wife, Elizabeth (1908); Thomas Barber (1950) and his first wife, Florence (1943); and John Booty (1979).

The churchyard was the scene of an impressive funeral in December 1916 when Private William Pegrum, aged 48, of the Ordnance Corps was laid to rest with military honours. Private Pegrum had enlisted in October 1915 but 12 months later he died in Portsmouth from pneumonia; 'The coffin was wrapped in the Union Jack [and] the cortege was headed by a bugler and a firing party of fourteen men from the Training Reserve Battalion, St Albans, and six privates from the same unit acted as bearers. It proceeded slowly through the village to the churchyard, a large number of silent and respectful sympathisers lining the route and the blinds of all dwellings being drawn...the firing party discharged three volleys over the open grave and the bugler sounded the "Last Post" with thrilling effect'[12]. Six servicemen of the Second World War are also interred in the churchyard.

At the present time the churchyard, now surrounded by housing and warehouse development, continues to be maintained by volunteers and, with preservation orders protecting the mature trees, a place of solitude and contemplation has been secured for the benefit of the community.

End notes
[1] Sir Edlyne Tomlin *The Law Dictionary Volume 1* 1835
[2] CERC: Correspondence 7 April 1826 31 f 432
[3] HALS: Conveyance DS1/31/1/72
[4] HALS: Petition DS1/31/1/72
[5] HALS: Declaration DS1/31/1/72
[6] HALS: File note 28 March 1934 DS1/31/1/72

[7] HALS: Documents, correspondence and following 3 paragraphs DS1/31/1/72

[8] CA: Statutory Declarations

[9] HALS: Policy document DSA1/17/12/19

[10] HALS: Instrument of Consecration DSA2/1/73

[11] John Cussans *History of Hertfordshire – Vol 3 Cassio Hundred 1881* p 39

[12] *Herts Advertiser* 6 December 1916

CHAPTER SEVEN

The Vicarage

Historically, the term vicarage described the office and income of a vicar but came to refer to the accommodation provided for him. Created as a perpetual curacy, the dwelling occupied by the minister at London Colney was more properly known by the general description of parsonage and was referred to as such by the first incumbent, Markland Barnard, in correspondence. In the latter half of the 19th century the status of perpetual curates became the equivalent of vicars and the dwelling could be described as a vicarage.

Thomas Newcome, the promoter of the chapel at London Colney, having embarked on the building project, turned his thoughts to the provision of suitable accommodation for the incoming minister. As with his original intention for the chapel, he first sought a property within his own parish of Shenley which extended to the banks of the River Colne. His diary entry of 1 September 1824 records that he had *'agreed to buy Colney Cottage for 700Gs [700 guineas - £735] - with view to a Ministers House of Residence'*[1]. In later maps[2] the property presently occupied (2010) by the Colney Fox Vintage Inn is identified as Colney Cottage. It seems that the sale was not completed because the survey undertaken in 1840 for the purposes of the Tithe Commutation Act of 1836 records that the unnamed property (*'House & yard'*) on the site is part of the Caledon estate and held by William Joseline. The dwelling was clearly considered of sufficient size and status to become the parsonage. At the time of the 1851 census *'Colney Cottage'* was occupied by the Roberts family of 5 adults attended by 4 domestic servants. By 1882 the property had become Tyttenhanger Lodge, a *'young gentlemen's boarding school'*[3] attracting pupils from home and overseas and which removed to Seaford, Sussex, in 1911.

Whatever the outcome of the negotiations for the purchase of Colney Cottage, 5 months later, in February 1825, Thomas Newcome acquired land and buildings abutting the site of the Chapel[4] (together with 2 smaller strips of land) adjacent to the Swan Public House described as:

All that brick messuage or tenement with the cottage thereto adjoining and belonging (part of which said cottage was lately a kitchen and other part thereof a coach house to the said messuage or tenement) And also the stable yard garden and other the premises to the said messuage or tenement and cottage belonging or appertaining On which said premises or on some part thereof three several messuages or tenements and premises formerly stood situate standing and being at London Colney in the parish of St Peter in the liberty of St Alban in the said county of Herts formerly in the tenure of Elizabeth Sorsby[?] afterwards of John Walker and now or late of William Fox which said premises contain in breadth from south to north in the front and east parts thereof respectively eighty three feet three inches of assize or thereabouts (little more or less) and in depth from east to west one hundred and two feet six inches of assize or thereabouts and besides and independent of the yard or area which is in front of the said messuage or tenement cottage and stable and is parted by a Chinese fence or railing from the road there And which said Premises were lately the estate and property of the said John Walker

The previous occupation and use of the property is somewhat uncertain and although the centenary booklet says '*It was at one time an inn and is said to have been called "The George Tap"*' current research has not discovered evidence to support the comment. It is somewhat surprising that there is no mention of an inn on the site (as might be expected in such descriptions identifying conveyed property) included within the detailed description of the conveying indenture.

Although the foundations of the chapel were set out in August 1824, nonetheless, the project was beset with delays and resolution of the various issues, particularly the endowment of the chapel, caused Thomas Newcome concerns with regard to the financial liabilities he had assumed. Without an adequate income, the appointed minister would be unable to pay rent for the dwelling and in letters to the Church Building Society[5] and the Bishop of London[6], Thomas Newcome explained, firstly, that the absence of an endowment '*would have forced Me to sell My House adjoining the Chapel*' and, further, that '*The House...and the adjoining (one purchase)...one has been kept empty for a year for Him [Markland Barnard, minister] and the other produces £15. They may be had from Me if required without loss or profit to Me by the purchase and the Chapel debt also repaid to me*'. When the difficulties had been overcome,

Bennett & Starling Ltd

1925 Vicarage and former coach house (left) and Church

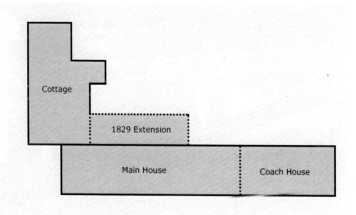

1830 Plan of Vicarage
(not to scale)

1829 Plan of ground floor extension

1829 Plan of first floor extension

and the chapel consecrated in July 1826, the property was offered to Markland Barnard, the appointed minister, '...*for no other Rent than such Services as may be compatible with due and prior duties of his Chapelry*'[7]. Three years later an application to purchase the property from Thomas Newcome was made to the Governors of Queen Anne's Bounty who were empowered to advance mortgage loans and grants towards the costs of improving parsonage houses at low rates of interest. The application was successful and by an indenture of 30 September 1829, evidencing the payment of £640 from the Governors to Thomas Newcome, the property was conveyed to the '*said Markland Barnard and his successors Curates of the Curacy of St Peter Colney aforesaid for ever for the perpetual augmentation of the same Curacy and to for and upon no other use trust and intent or purpose whatsoever*'[8].

The parsonage comprised a 3 storey dwelling with adjoining coach house and a cottage at the rear, set at right angles, created a separate wing. At the time of the conveyance the Governors of Queen Anne's Bounty also agreed to fund additions to the property comprising a 2 storey extension adjoining the main dwelling and rear wing in order to provide a dining room on the ground floor and an additional bedroom on the upper level together with alterations to the existing accommodation[9]. Benjamin Fowler, surveyor of St Albans, drew up a detailed specification and by a sworn statement of 1 October 1829, John Bisney, '*of Colney in the County of Herts, Builder*' undertook to complete the works in '*a good, substantial and workmanlike manner...on or before the first day of March, One thousand eight hundred and Thirty*' for the sum of £362 14s 4d.

An evocative description of the parsonage appears in the 1925 centenary booklet:

> The staircases wander up and down with charming waywardness, and most of the doors are well provided with bolts and bars. There is an abundance of dressing rooms and cupboards. The lower part of it, built on in the direction of the church, is called "The Cottage." In the time of the former Vicar [Markland Barnard], it served as stable and coachhouse, and as a dwelling for the coachman, while one room was used as a study. By pulling down of a partition wall this has now been united with the "Cottage kitchen" to form a room for parish purposes. The village library is kept here. The rest of the cottage is used for purposes very necessary in a Vicarage, for

the storage of articles to be sold at jumble sales or at the missionary sale of work held annually in the Vicarage garden.

On taking up occupation Reverend Markland Barnard arranged to insure the property and the policy records of the Sun Fire Office for 1834 provide the following details[10]:

Sun Fire Office 1834	
Description	Sum Insured
On his dwelling house Kitchen and washhouse all communicating situate as aforesaid	£750
Household Goods fixtures wearing apparel printed books and plate therein	£500
House stable and Coachhouse all adjoining to each other up to the above mentioned in occupation of Pridmore*	£250
All brick and slate	£1500

*The occupier Pridmore may have been the coachman.

The accommodation provided was substantial and sufficient for the large household of Markland Barnard which, at times, comprised 13 family members and domestic staff:

Census Records		
Census	Vicarage household	Domestic Staff
1851	5 (Markland Barnard)	Cook, housemaid, footman
1861	8*	Lady's maid, footman, cook, housemaid, nurse
1871	9*	Footman, lady's maid, housemaid, nurse
1881	4*	Footman, housemaid, cook
1891	3	Cook, housemaid
1901	4 (Thomas Bluett)	Cook, housemaid
1911	2	2 female servants

• includes the families of his children living at the vicarage with Markland Barnard

The employment of domestic staff should be viewed within the perspective of the priest's status in the community at the time and compared with the household of local mansions. For example, the 1851 census records that at Tyttenhanger House and Colney House (now the site of the Pastoral Centre in Shenley) households of 4 (including 2 visitors) and 2 persons respectively were attended by retinues of up to 16 servants.

Ken Barker

2009 The Vicarage

Ken Barker

2009 Remains of cellars in Vicarage garden

A national survey of all land and property in England and Wales was carried out under the Finance Act of 1910 which imposed a levy on the increase in value of land that had accrued since April 1909 and the date of subsequent sale. Several years were spent on the valuation process but the tax was repealed in 1920. For the purposes of the Act the vicarage site was valued at £1,000[11].

After providing accommodation for the incumbents of St Peter's Church and their families for over 100 years a decision was taken to replace the rambling vicarage with a smaller, more manageable, dwelling. Once again the Governor's of Queen Anne's Bounty provided assistance and in March 1930 advanced a mortgage loan of £315 at an interest rate of 4% towards the costs which was finally discharged in July 1950[12]. The new house of neo-Georgian design was completed in May 1930 with the accommodation comprising 4 bedrooms, dressing room, bathroom, 2 reception rooms, kitchen scullery, pantry, hall and cloakroom. After demolition, however, traces of the original vicarage remain and the vaulted ceilings of the old cellars of the property are visible in the vicarage garden together with the flint and brick garden wall.

End notes
[1] HALS: *Family Register of Thomas Newcome* ACC 2800
[2] Ordnance Survey 1878
[3] Kelly's Directory 1882
[4] CA: Recited in conveyance 20 September 1829
[5] LPL: Correspondence 24 July 1826 ICBS 00463
[6] CERC: Correspondence 7 April FP Howley 31 f 432-44v
[7] LPL: Correspondence 24 July 1826 ICBS 00463
[8] CA: Indenture 30 September 1829
[9] CERC: Plan & specification QAB/7/6/E15
[10] LMA: Policy records MS11936/1172290
[11] HALS: Map IR1/421 Register IR2/65/3-4
[12] HALS: Mortgage Deed DP93B-3-5

CHAPTER EIGHT

The Parish Centre

Over the years a variety of venues have been used for church meetings and other related activities. After the retirement of Reverend Markland Barnard in 1892, the coach house annexe of the old vicarage was no longer required for stabling and staff accommodation. The centenary booklet explains that a meeting room for *'parish purposes'* was created by pulling down an internal wall with the remainder of the building used for storage. After demolition of the vicarage in 1930 a small hall (15 ft x 35 ft) of brick, iron and asbestos sheeting was erected to the north-east of the church for use as a choir vestry but was available for meetings too. Later, when the church school in the High Street closed in 1949, part of the building became the parish hall until its demolition circa 1978.

The need for a permanent building to serve the needs of the church and the wider community was well recognised. Following the arrival of Michael Beer as the incumbent of St Peter's Church in 1980 a decision was taken to embark on the largest fundraising and building project since the church was established in London Colney 155 years earlier. Fundraising and building committees were convened and an architect was instructed. The proposals envisaged a parish centre on the site of the demolished 1930 building and having a physical link to the church. Alternative plans were considered for accommodation comprising a hall, parish office, choir vestry, kitchen and toilets but raising funds for the estimated building costs of £60,000 presented an immense task.

Whilst fundraising efforts continued action was taken to provide temporary accommodation. In 1980 a portable building, previously used as a class room, was acquired at cost of £2,115 some of which was met by the trustees of the Caledon Estate. A fraught day was experienced when the 4 sections of the portable building were lifted over the church suspended from the jib of a mobile crane and positioned on a concrete slab foundation constructed by church volunteers to the north-east of the church. After the sections were bolted together work commenced to remove the traces of its former use and to decorate and furnish the

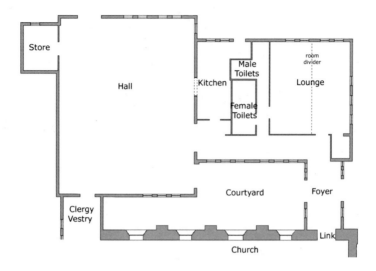

Approved plan of Parish Centre

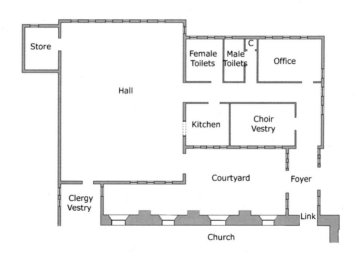

Alternative plan of Parish Centre

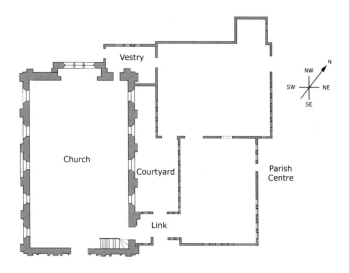

Plan of connections to Church

room. A toilet and small kitchen were installed. When sufficient funds, including a grant from the Diocese of St Albans, were available construction of the parish centre commenced with the labour provided by members of a youth experience training scheme organised by the Diocese.

In May 1983, the temporary building was removed and the site cleared. The foundations were excavated and by August 1983 the concrete floor slab had been formed after which construction of the walls began. In January 1984 bad weather interrupted work but March witnessed the completion of the external and internal walls permitting the erection of the roof trusses. By June the link with the church had been finished and completion of the roof in July enabled internal fitting out works to begin. Over the winter of 1984-85 the electric wiring was installed and the kitchen and toilets fitted. The architect, Michael Meacher, fashioned a Taize style cross of white stone and slate that was donated to the project and incorporated into the front gable end of the roof. Much of the finishing interior decoration was undertaken by parishioners and completed only a few hours before the service of thanksgiving and dedication of the new parish centre was conducted by the Right Reverend John Taylor, Bishop of St Albans on 18 July 1985.

John Webb

1983 Temporary portable building

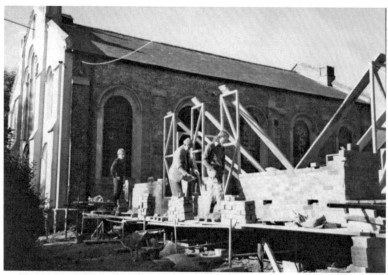

John Webb

1983 Parish centre under construction

Ken Barker

2010 View of Parish Centre from churchyard

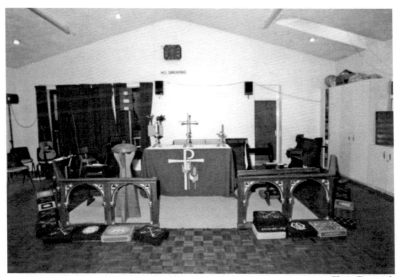

Chris Emerick

1996 Parish Centre used for services during
internal redecoration of church

By 1995 there was a realisation that the arrangement of the parish centre required to be more flexible in order to meet the needs of the parish and hirers of the facilities. Alternative solutions were considered including an extension either externally to the hall or at first floor level over the parish office and kitchen areas. In the event, a decision was made to take down the wall separating the choir vestry and parish office and to install a folding partition. The cost of the alterations incurred a significant saving on the other proposals and a versatile room for committee meetings, training sessions and a crèche during services was created. An important function of the centre has the use of the hall for services when the church has been unavailable because of re-ordering and maintenance works. In a recent survey it was estimated that 25,000 people visited the parish centre each year demonstrating the immense benefit that it has provided to the community.

CHAPTER NINE

Ministers of St Peter's Church

In the 185 year history of St Peter's Church (up to 2010) there have been 7 officiating ministers:

Ministers			
Name	Incumbency	Duration	Age at retirement
Markland Barnard (1803-1895)	1826-1893	67 years	89
Thomas Bluett (1855-1937)	1893-1927	34 years	72
Thomas Barber (1873-1950)	1928-1948	20 years	75
John Booty (1904-1996)	1949-1979	30 years	75
Michael Beer (b 1944)	1980-1997	17 years	-
Hilary Derham (b 1950)	1998-2003	5 years	-
Lynne Fawns (b 1956)	2003 -	-	-

The first 2 incumbents, Markland Barnard and Thomas Bluett, had a combined service to the community of over 100 years and were typical ministers of that period; both came from middle class backgrounds and were educated at private grammar schools before entering colleges at Cambridge University. At the time, the '...universities were largely seminaries for Anglican clergy...[and]...in 1830, 50.1 per cent of those who matriculated at Cambridge were subsequently ordained'[1]. In later years it was the more usual practice for ordination candidates to attend theological colleges.

MARKLAND BARNARD 1803-1895 (Ministry 1826 -1892)

Markland Barnard was the son of Robert Barnard, a long serving employee of the East India Company and a member of the Worshipful Company of Mercers, the senior City of London livery company. The Barnard family had been associated with the livery company since the reign of Henry IV in the fifteenth century and Robert Barnard, representing the thirteenth generation, held the position of Master Warden in 1813. He retired at the early age of 51 in 1820 when his position of assistant Coast and Surat warehouse-keeper was abolished and an annual pension of £1,000 was granted by the East Indian Company amid some controversy[2]. The centenary booklet mentions that, during his latter years, Robert Barnard lived in London Colney where he died in February 1845 and was interred in the churchyard of St Peter's Church.

The Mercers' Company supported St Paul's School by way of a charitable foundation and Markland Barnard, born in 1803, attended as a pupil and became school captain[3] before studying at Trinity College, Cambridge. By 1825, before graduation, he was engaged to Emma Gwynne whose brother was curate at All Hallows, Tottenham, assisting the vicar, Thomas Newcome, also rector of Shenley and promoter of the chapel at London Colney. Philip, 3rd Earl of Hardwicke, patron of the new chapel, entrusted the nomination of the first minister to Thomas Newcome who, in December 1825, sponsored Markland Barnard although he was not yet ordained in holy orders. Shenley was within the diocese of Lincoln and graduating with a Bachelor of Arts degree in February 1826, the same month he was ordained by the Bishop of Lincoln at St Mary-le-Bone Chapel in London[4]. He was first licensed as a stipendary curate to the parish of Shenley and, in December 1826, as perpetual curate of St Peter's Chapel, London Colney[5].

Two years after his arrival at London Colney, Markland Barnard married Emma Gwynne in May 1828 at All Hallows in Tottenham. A daughter, Emma, was born in 1830 and a son, Markland junior, in 1832. Emma married Henry Yates in 1856 and Markland junior married Henry's sister, Frances Yates in 1859. Henry and Frances were the children of William Yates, an army officer, and both Henry Yates and Markland junior embarked on military careers. The younger Markland was an officer in the West Kent Militia and for several years was a member of the Honourable Corps of Gentlemen-of-Arms, the official bodyguard of the sovereign on state occasions[6]. The centenary booklet also reports that the '*son of Rev. Markland Barnard...was at one time well known in the hunting field in this neighbourhood and kept several horses for hunting with various stables in Colney.*' The son-in-law, Henry Yates, was an officer in the Royal Artillery. The census records of 1861, 1871 and 1881 have the families of both Barnard children resident at London Colney suggesting that the vicarage was used as their family home when the respective families did not accompany the husband on his military duties.

In the Religious Survey of Hertfordshire produced in 1848 by

William Upton, a non conformist minster, the ministry of 'Revd M Barnard' at the London Colney 'Episcopal Chapel' was described as 'Amiable, dull and inefficient'[7]. The pastoral duties of Markland Barnard increased in 1832 when, in addition to his duties at London Colney, he became vicar of St Margaret's Church at Ridge and, again, in 1863 when he was appointed as Rural Dean for Barnet. He was also domestic chaplain to members of the Caledon family and his responsibilities extended beyond these clerical duties. He was appointed a Land Tax Commissioner in 1836[8] and continued his family's association with the Mercers' livery company. The centenary history describes how Markland Barnard 'used to drive in his carriage to London for the meetings of the Company every Friday. At one time he used frequently to walk to London.' Like his father, he became Master Warden in 1863 and during the year of office presided over a ceremony to present the freedom of the Company to the Prince of Wales, later Edward VII. After the proceedings he entertained the royal guest in the Council Chamber[9]. The following year he gave evidence on behalf of St Paul's School to a Parliamentary Commission[10].

Emma died in early 1893 and the same year Markland Barnard retired after an incumbency that had lasted for 67 years. In retirement he moved to Galley Dean, near Chelmsford, where his son was living. He died there on 15 February 1895 aged 92 and was interred in the family vault in St Peter's churchyard.

THOMAS BLUETT 1855-1937 (Ministry 1893-1927)

Thomas Lovell Bluett came from a clerical family and at the time of his birth in 1855, his father, John Bluett, was a curate in Yalding, Kent. Later John Bluett moved to a similar position at Dengie, near Chelmsford, and at the age of 15 Thomas was a boarder at Felstead Grammar School near Dunmow. He went on to study at St John's College, Cambridge, and graduated with a Bachelor of Arts degree in 1877 before taking holy orders. After his ordination in 1880 Thomas Bluett served as curate at Holy Trinity, Exeter (1880-1882), St Peter, Norbiton (1882-1883) and Southchurch (1883-1893) before his appointment to St Peter's Church, London Colney.

In 1882 Thomas Bluett married Elizabeth Cock, the daughter of a Norfolk farmer, and their son, Thomas Lovell Chapman Bluett, was born in 1884. Thomas junior became active in local affairs, becoming Honorary Secretary of the London Colney Horticultural Society, and responsible for the booklet describing the history of St Peter's Church, London Colney, published in 1925 as part of the church centenary celebrations[11]. Elizabeth died in 1908 and was interred in the churchyard. Two years later, in 1910, Thomas married his second wife Elizabeth Bodger.

Thomas Bluett was described as being '*Of pronounced evangelical views*'[12] and during periods of his ministry members of the Church Army were assigned to the church. A parishioner recalls her mother commenting that '*...when the old vicar was there (Mr Bluett) you had to be early for a Sermon or you wouldn't get a seat. You'd have to stand at the back*'. His ministry witnessed many changes including the re-seating and renovation of the church, the Church Lads Brigade was established and the church school enlarged. Of particular importance was the enhanced status of St Peter's Church in 1909 following the creation of the consolidated chapelry. On his retirement in 1927 parishioners presented Thomas Bluett with a chiming clock and 2 armchairs[13]. He moved to Worthing where he died on 9 January 1937 and his remains were returned to London Colney and laid to rest with those of his first wife.

THOMAS VERNON BARBER 1873-1950 (Ministry 1928-1948)

Thomas Vernon Hollingsworth Barber, the youngest son of William Barber, was born in Cambridge in 1873. By the age of 17 he was working as an insurance clerk in London but in the census of 1901 and 1911 Thomas Barber is described as a hat manufacturer and employer having married his first wife, Florence Smith, in 1903. During that time Thomas was involved in lay pastoral work and later wrote in the December 1940 issue of St Peter's Parish Magazine appealing for toys for the children in the '*slum parish of St Mary's, Somer's Town, N.W. It was in this parish that I worked as a layman before I took holy orders and I have a great affection for it.*' There was an abrupt change of career when he was admitted to Christ College, Cambridge, and graduated with an arts degree in 1922 at the age of 49. After further studies at Westcott House theological college in Cambridge, Thomas Barber was ordained in 1922 and served as curate at St Paul's Church in Tottenham until 1928 when he was appointed to London Colney. The same year he also became Officiating Chaplain at the recently opened Middlesex

Colony Mental Hospital later to be known as Harperbury Hospital.

His wife, Florence Barber, was active in the community and supported the local branches of the Mothers' Union and the British Legion becoming president of the Women's Section. Following her death in 1943 members of the both associations subscribed towards memorials in her name. In September 1945, at the age of 72, Thomas Barber married for second time. His bride was Mrs Mabel Lediard the matron of the Middlesex Colony Hospital responsible for the welfare of the 1,200 patients and a prominent member of the nursing profession[14]. The ceremony at London Colney was conducted by the Bishop of St Albans and the British Journal of Nursing reported that '...*the atmosphere was suffused with harmonious affection*'; further commenting, in recognition of the recent cessation of World War 2 hostilities, that '*In the midst of the wreckage and misery of war, surely we ought to have deep sense of thankfulness that such things as hope and love assert themselves like roses blooming among the ruins*'.

Mabel Barber was a friend and professional colleague of Ethel Bedford-Fenwick nee Manson (1857-1947) who had become internationally known for her campaigns promoting the structured training and registration of nurses which were successfully implemented on the enactment of the Nurses Act 1919. Ethel Bedford-Fenwick had been enrolled as the first state registered nurse and, arguably, had had a greater influence on the progress of the nursing profession than Florence Nightingale (1820-1910) who had opposed the campaigns. Her health deteriorated following a fall in 1946 and she moved into the vicarage at London Colney, to be cared for by her friend, Mabel Barber, where she died in March 1947[15].

The style of Thomas Barber's ministry differed from that of his evangelical predecessor and was regarded by some parishioners as '*High church*'[16]. It was during his incumbency that a chantry screen (1930) was erected separating the chancel from the nave and a gift of a chalice (1929) from the Confraternity of the Blessed Sacrament, an anglo-catholic organisation, was accepted. He retired to Westcliff-on-Sea in poor health in 1948 undergoing an operation in April 1950, from which he never fully recovered[17], and died 2 months later on 25 June 1950. Thomas Barber was interred in the churchyard of St Peter's next to his first wife.

Markland Barnard
(Ministry 1826-1893)

Thomas Bluett
(Ministry 1893-1927)

Thomas Barber
(Ministry 1928-1948)

John Booty
(Ministry 1949-1979)

Michael Beer
(Ministry 1980-1997)

Jan Beer
(Curate 1987-1997)

Hilary Derham
(Ministry 1998-2003)

Lynne Fawns
(Ministry 2003-)

JOHN BOOTY 1904-1996 (Ministry 1949-1979)

John Robert Booty was born in St Pancras, London, in 1904 and upon leaving school entered the insurance industry before studying for holy orders and graduating as a Theological Associate of King's College, London, in 1931. Ordained the same year he served as curate at St Luke, Walthamstow (1931-33), St Mary Magdelane, Colchester (1933-36) and in Houghton Regis before being appointed vicar of St Peter's Church, London Colney, in 1949. Following his predecessor, John Booty became chaplain at Harperbury Hospital. On retirement in 1979 he moved to Bricket Wood where he died in 1996. There was a daughter, Dora, from his marriage to Ruby.

A man of strong principles, John Booty 'signed the pledge' to abstain from alcohol as a youth and was a conscientious objector during World War 2. He was instrumental in establishing the 'Meals on Wheels' service in London Colney and as a keen musician promoted the choir at St Peter's Church. During his incumbency, John Booty was often consulted by the local authority to suggest names for new roads in London Colney commemorating local individuals.

MICHAEL BEER b 1944 (Ministry 1980-1997)

Michael Beer was born in 1944 and entered Chichester Theological College in 1966. After ordination in 1969 and serving as curate in Leagrave he undertook missionary work in St Vincent, one of the Caribbean Windward islands until 1974 thereafter returning to the UK as curate of Holy Trinity church in Bishops Stortford. Appointed vicar of St Peter's Church, London Colney, in 1980, it was under the leadership of Michael Beer that the ambitious plans to re-order the church and build a permanent parish centre were realised. His incumbency came to an end in 1997 when he was appointed vicar of Northaw & Cuffley and he retired from the living in 2009.

During his ministry at London Colney Michael Beer was assisted by his wife, Jan, and the Reverend Rudolph (Rudi) Heinze. Michael Beer married Jan in December 1968 and their sons Simon and Matthew spent their formative years at the vicarage. Jan Beer had obtained teaching qualifications at Goldsmiths College, London, in 1964 and later studied at Oak Hill Theological College,

Southgate, graduating in 1983. Awarded a Diploma in Social Services in 1986 she was ordained in 1987 and served as Honorary Curate at St Peter's Church until 1997. Jan Beer was appointed chaplain of St Albans High School for Girls and then served at Middlesex University from 1994. After 1997 Jan acted as a non stipendary minister at her husband's parish of Northaw & Cuffley. Both Michael and Jan Beer are accomplished musicians and services at St Peter's Church were enlivened with their musical interludes.

Rudi Heinze graduated from Concordia College (USA), founded by the Evangelical Lutheran Church of America, in 1956 with a Bachelor of Science degree, acquiring a Master of Arts qualification at the De Paul University (1959) and a doctorate from the University of Iowa. After teaching at the Universities of Iowa, Illinois, Ohio State, and Concordia he moved to the UK in 1986 taking up a lectureship at Oak Hill Theological College in Southgate, North London, and becoming Vice Principal in 1994. He was ordained in 1986 and was appointed a non stipendary minister of St Peter's Church, London Colney. In addition to his academic and clerical duties Rudi is the author of several books and presented programmes for BBC television. He returned to the USA in 1999.

HILARY DERHAM b 1950 (Ministry 1998-2003)

The appointment of Hilary Derham as vicar of London Colney broke with tradition in more ways than one. Not only was Hilary the first female priest and appointed as a priest-in-charge rather than a permanent incumbent but also she was the first vicar of St Peter's Church not to have a surname beginning with the letter B! Born in 1950 Hilary studied at Nottingham University, graduated as a Bachelor of Pharmacy in 1971 and worked for the Bloomsbury Health Authority in London before entering Chichester Theological College in 1989. Ordination followed in 1991 and there was service at Holy Trinity, Stevenage, as Parish Deacon and Curate before her appointment to London Colney. Hilary became a governor of Bowmansgreen primary school. Ill health caused her premature retirement in 2003.

LYNNE FAWNS b 1956 (Ministry 2003-)

The present incumbent, Lynne Fawns (nee Ramsden), was born in 1956 in Hull and on leaving school entered the nursing profession qualifying as a State Registered Nurse in 1977 and specialising in Pyschogeriatic Assessment at the London and Mount Pleasant Hospitals in London. She married Martyn Fawns in 1977 and her nursing career was interrupted by the births of Benjamin in 1981 and Rebecca in 1983. Lynne decided to continue her education as a mature student and graduated from Thames Valley University in 1995 with a Bachelor of Arts (Honours) degree. Called to the ministry she studied on the North Thames Ministerial Training Course and following ordination in 2000 was appointed curate at All Saints, Hillingdon. Lynne was appointed to St Peter's Church, London Colney, in December 2003. She is a vocations officer for the Diocese of St Albans and a governor of Bowmansgreen primary school.

End notes

[1] W M Jacob *The Clerical Profession in the Long Eighteenth Century 168-1840* Oxford University Press 2007 ISBN 978-0-19-921300-9 p45

[2] *The Asiatic Journal and Monthly Register for British India and its Dependencies* Black, Kingsbury, Parbury & Allen 1820 p 461 *et seq*

[3] *The Standard* 22 July 1880

[4] *Quarterly Theological Review 1826* C & J Rivington Volume III p 529

[5] www.theclergydatabase.org.uk/index.html

[6] *Hart's Annual Army List, Militia List, and Imperial Yeomanry List* J Murray 1863 p 123

[7] *Religion in Hertfordshire 1847-1851* Hertfordshire Record Society 1995 p 69

[8] *A Collection of Public General Statues Passed in 1836* Eyre & Spottiswoode p 617

[9] James Maculay *Speeches And Addresses of HRH The Prince of Wales 1863-1888* John Murray [reprinted by Kessinger Publishing Legacy Reprints] p 16

[10] *Report of Her Majesty's Commissioners appointed to enquire into the Revenues and Management of Certain Colleges and Schools* HMSO 1864 p 71 *et seq*

[11] *Herts Advertiser & St Albans Times* Obituary 15 January 1937

[12] ibid

[13] ibid

[14] *The British Journal of Nursing* September 1945 p 104

[15] ibid April 1947 p 42

[16] Margaret Hopkins November 2008

[17] *Herts Advertiser & St Albans Times* Obituary 30 June 1950

CHAPTER TEN

How Ministers Were Paid

O ver many generations, and continuing today, the remuneration of the clergy has been a matter of debate and concern. Some parishes were wealthy, with the incumbent enjoying a significant income, whilst many others were in more straitened circumstances. At the time that St Peter's Church, London Colney, was established the income of a minster came from a number of sources including endowments, glebe rents, offerings, pew rents, Queen Anne's Bounty and tithes. It was the manner in which ministers were remunerated that promoted resistance to the creation of ecclesiastical districts within existing parishes because of the resultant loss of income arising from a decrease in the size of the parish and the number of parishioners attending the parish church.

Sources of Income

Endowment	Philip, 3rd Earl of Hardwicke, who had provided the land for the church, became patron of the chapelry and endowed the annual sum of £40. However, writing in 1850[1], the first incumbent, Reverend Markland Barnard, commented that about 5 years earlier the trust created under the endowment deed had been transferred to the Governors of the Queen Anne's Bounty and, presumably, the income therefrom was subsumed within the grants paid from the Bounty fund.
Glebe land	acquired either by endowment or purchase, could be cultivated or rented out for the benefit of the incumbent.

In 1843 a site extending to 4½ acres *'formerly called Townsend field but now more usually known by the name of Crouch field'*, and a short distance northwest of the church, was conveyed by Catherine, Countess of Caledon, for the nominal sum of 10 shillings [50p] to the Governors of Queen Anne's Bounty[2] to be set aside as glebe in order to augment the income of St Peter's. The conveyance may have regularised an existing arrangement because the Tithe Survey carried out 3 years earlier in 1840 records the Reverend Markland

Barnard as the owner of the field given over to 'Cottage Allotment' ['an allotment of a small portion of land to a country labourer for garden cultivation']. Laid out in plots which were rented to around 60 allotment holders, the glebe land produced an annual rental income of £10.

Over time parts of the glebe land were given over to other uses and, for example, parcels were transferred to the neighbouring church school.

During the later 19th century there were independent movements, particularly amongst the Christian community, to provide a proper environment for the spiritual and physical development of children and adolescents whose opportunity for such improvement typically ceased after they had left school at an early age. Known as the 'Brigade Movement' the efforts of the initiators resulted in the founding of the Boys' Brigade in 1883 followed by the Gordon Boys' Brigade (after General Gordon of Khartoum renown) in 1885. In 1891 the Church Lads' Brigade was formed and, amalgamating with the Gordon Boys' Brigade, a national Anglican organisation was established. A troop was formed in London Colney under the auspices of St Peter's Church and in 1900 a 'Church Lads' Brigade Iron Room' was erected on the glebe land adjacent to the village school. By the mid 1930s the building was being used as an overflow classroom[3].

In 1906 a small washhouse was built on the land.

Offerings
: by tradition the minister was entitled to the offerings of the Easter church collections.

Pew rent
: was income from advantageously placed sittings in the church rented to parishioners. Free sittings were available for the poor and it was a condition of the grant advanced by the Church Building Society towards the building costs that 50% of the sittings at St Peter's Church, London Colney, be provided free of charge. Pew rents were being collected until 1929.

Queen Anne's Bounty
: was established in 1704 to augment the incomes of poorer clergy with capital sums advanced to enable land to be purchased in order to provide an in income

for the parish and, later, for the building and repairing vicarages. From the early 19th century the fund was supplemented by Parliamentary grants distributed under the auspices of the Fund Commissioners.

At the time that St Peter's Chapel was built in 1825 the qualifying threshold for funding from Queen Anne's Bounty was an annual income under £200 which was well above the declared value of £65 for the chapelry. Between 1826 and 1834 payments made to St Peter's Church, London Colney, from Parliamentary grants, under the auspices of the Commissioners of Queen Anne's Bounty, totalled £1,000[4], which may have included the purchase of the vicarage in 1829 from Thomas Newcome for £640.

Tithes   were levied on the produce of the land. Rectors received the benefit of great (or rectorial) tithes raised on corn, grain and wood with the vicar entitled to the proceeds of small (or vicarial) tithes from other produce. Under the terms of the Tithe Commutation Act of 1836 payments in kind were commuted into a monetary equivalent and rent-charge.

As a perpetual curate, however, the minister of St Peter's Church, London Colney, was not entitled to the receive the tithe income of its chapelry district which remained due to the mother church.

It was not unusual for incumbents to remain serving ministers until either age or ill health prevented them from carrying out their pastoral duties. Markland Barnard, the first minister at London Colney, served for 67 years and retired in 1893 at the age of 89. In addition to devotion to their vocational calling there were the considerations of secured income and tenure. Clerical pensions were not introduced until the Clergy Pension Measure of 1926 and previously, under certain circumstances, a retiring minister could be awarded ⅓ of the income of the living[5] which was not popular with the succeeding incumbent. In order to increase income it became a common practice for a minister to hold the living of more than one parish (and in some cases several parishes) assisted by paid curates. Abuses of the system were addressed by the Pluralities Act of 1838 which limited incumbency to not more than 2 parishes within a 10 mile radius (reduced to 3 miles in 1850).

Local examples of plurality were Thomas Newcome, Rector of Shenley, who was appointed vicar of All Hallows, Tottenham, in 1824 and Markland Barnard.

Markland Barnard was a bachelor when appointed perpetual curate at St Peter's Church, London Colney, in 1826 but by 1832 he was married with 2 children and concerned with the level of his income. The neighbouring parish of Ridge, also administered by the Diocese of London and sponsored by Philip, 3rd Earl of Hardwicke, was far wealthier and the annual income of £190 declared in 1835 was 3 times that of London Colney at £65[6]. When the incumbency of St Margaret's Church at Ridge fell vacant in 1832 Markland Barnard was appointed the vicar in addition to his duties at London Colney. At first it is apparent that he attempted to administer both parishes himself thus avoiding the expense of a curate's stipend but this did not meet with the approval of the Bishop of London who wrote in December 1832[7] that, *'I cannot consent that a parish [Ridge], where there has been up to the present time, a resident Clergyman, and double duty [two services on Sunday], should henceforth be without a resident Incumbent or Curate and have only single duty, and that too at an hour by no means convenient to the parishioners...I am quite aware how inadequate your income is at Colney Hatch [sic], and that you have no means of increasing it but by taking pupils, but I am obliged to look at the spiritual provision to be made for a parish rather than to the interests of individual Clergymen'.*

Seemingly, the issue of the curate was not resolved until 1839 partly because of the reluctance of Markland Barnard to pay the recommended curate's stipend of £100 causing the Bishop to write to him in March 1839[8] *'I heartily wish that Ridge and Colney were much more valuable than they are but the law is peremptory which requires me to fix £100 as the stipend where the population exceeds 300, even though the whole income of the benefice does not exceed that value. The special & peculiar cases in which the Bishop is allowed to assign a smaller stipend are not cases where the incumbent has another Living but where he is aged & infirm & is obliged to have a Curate'.* In the event, Anthony Gower was appointed curate at Ridge and, residing in the vicarage, served for almost 40 years.

By 1866 the annual income of London Colney chapelry had increased to £120[9]. The following year (1867) the income of the living was addressed by the Ecclesiastical Commissioners established by Act of Parliament in 1836 with extensive powers to improve the administration of the Church of England. These powers included the ability to make financial provision *'for the cure of souls in parishes where such assistance is most required'*. The Commissioners considered whether certain tithe rents formerly due to the Bishop of Ely, patron of St Peter's Church, St Albans, should be appropriated for the benefit of St Peter's, London Colney. Three proposals were offered for consideration[10]:

> 1. the substitution of tithe rent charge for the grant of £8 per annum at present made by the Commissioners to the benefice.
> 2. the sale of tithe rent charge to Queen Anne's Bounty in consideration of the payment to the Commissioners of the Capital monies held by them to the credit of the Cure and producing £79.0.0 per annum.
> 3. the augmentation of the benefice with tithe rent charge producing £91.0.0. per annum conditionally upon such augmentation being met with an equivalent benefaction from non-ecclesiastical sources.

Each proposal was accompanied by a schedule prepared for the purposes of the Tithe Commutation Act describing the ownership, occupation, acreage of the land concerned together with the rent charges. Proposal no. 2 was agreed and is reflected in later declarations of annual income made by the incumbents to the diocese[11].

Income 1887-1931							
	1887	1905	1910	1914	1921	1929	1931
Tithe	Nil	Nil	Nil	Nil	Nil	Nil	Nil
Glebe Land	£10	£10	£10	£10	£10	£10	£8
Ecclesiastical Commissioners	£8	£8	£97	£105	£207	£279	£279
Queen Anne's Bounty	£79	£79	£79	£79	£79	£79	£79
Pew Rents	£18	£8	£8	£8	£8	£8	Nil
Offerings	£12	£12	£12	£12	£12	£12	£10
Total	£127	£117	£206	£214	£316	£388	£376

In more recent times the position has been gradually regularised. Tithe rent charges were abolished by the Tithe Act 1936 and in 1948 Queen Anne's Bounty was merged with the Ecclesiastical Commissioners to create the Church Commissioners. Later, in 1978, under the terms of the Endowments and Glebe Measure of 1976, glebe land ceased to belong to individual incumbents and was transferred to the ownership of the local Diocesan Board of Finance which also receives the income from fees (marriage, burial etc). The intention was to ensure that glebe income was more fairly distributed amongst the clergy and the payment of stipends is now made centrally by the Church Commissioners although the financial burden falling upon congregations in support of the ministry has not diminished. The Diocesan Board levies a 'parish share' on each parish in order to raise some 75% of the diocesan expenditure on stipends and administration. The 'share' is calculated by a pre-determined formula. In 2009 the quota for St Peter's, London Colney, assessed at £34,000, was met by fundraising and gift aiding by members of the congregation. The 'parish share' does not include the fundraising necessary for the upkeep and maintenance of the church building.

End notes

[1] HALS: Letter D/ECd/Q2

[2] CA: Conveyance 26 July 1843

[3] Margaret Hopkins – memories 1997

[4] *Supplement to the Account of the Augmentation of Small Livings* 1835 Christopher Hodgson

[5] Incumbents Registration Act 1871

[6] *Liber Ecclesiastical – An Authentic Statement of the Revenues of the Established Church* 1835 Hamilton, Adams & Co

[7] LPL: Correspondence FP Blomfield 5 f 37

[8] LPL: Correspondence FP Blomfield 19 f 97

[9] *Clergy List* 1866

[10] HALS: Correspondence DP93B/3/2

[11] HALS: Terriers 1887-1931 DP3B/3/8

CHAPTER ELEVEN

The Village School

In addition to attending to the spiritual needs of the community, the clergy of St Peter's Church were associated with the introduction of education to London Colney. Until the 19th century a formal education was typically the privilege of those fortunate enough to be to able to pay. Amongst the less well-off there was a reluctance to release children for educational purposes because reliance was placed on the earnings that they could contribute to the income of the household. There were movements to broaden the availability of education and in 1811 the National Society for Promoting the Education of the Poor in the Principles of the Established Church (the National Society) was established with the laudable aim of promoting the foundation of a school in every parish in close association with the Church of England. From 1836 onwards legislation (School Sites Act 1836 et seq) facilitated the provision of sites for schools under which manorial common or waste land could be granted for educational purposes subject to the proviso that the land could revert to the original owner should such usage cease. Later in the century, the 1870 Education Act established Local School Boards responsible for providing elementary education thus creating a dual system with the National Church Schools scheme. School attendance for every child was made compulsory under subsequent acts and the leaving age was increased from the age of 10 years to 12 years by 1899 and 14 years by 1918.

In the 1834 Visitation Report of the Rural Dean[1] he makes references to a Sunday school attracting 64 pupils in London Colney and a daily school at Broad Colney open daily between 9 am and 2 pm attended by 26 scholars and funded by annual voluntary contributions of £40. By the end of the decade a strip of manorial waste land with a frontage onto the London Road had been provided by the Caledon family for the site of a school at London Colney. There is reference to the school land in a subsequent indenture[2] of 1843 when Catherine, Dowager Countess of Caledon, widow of the Du Pre, 2nd Earl of Caledon, who had died in April 1839, conveyed 4 acres neighbouring the school site, for use as glebe land in support of the church, *'abutting towards the west upon the School House erected by the late Earl of Caledon upon a parcel of waste ground lying between the said field and the London Road and the Ground and premises thereto belonging'*.

An application was made in January 1839 for union with the National Society signed by Elizabeth, Dowager Countess of Hardwicke, Henry Hoyle Oddie (owner of Colney House formerly on the site of the Pastoral Centre in Shenley Lane) and Markland Barnard (perpetual curate of St Peter's Church, London Colney):

APPLICATION FOR UNION

It is the wish of those that have the management of the Daily and Sunday Schools at London Colney near Barnet in the County of Hertford in the Diocese of London that the same should be united to the NATIONAL SOCIETY, FOR PROMOTING THE EDUCATION OF THE POOR IN THE PRINCIPLES OF THE ESTABLISHED CHURCH THROUGHOUT ENGLAND AND WALES.

In these Schools the National System of teaching will be adopted as far as is practicable; the Children will be instructed in the Liturgy and Catechism of the Establish Church, and constantly attend Divine Service at their Parish Church, or other place of Worship under the Establishment, as far as possible, on the Lord's Day; unless such reasons be assigned for their non-attendance, as shall be satisfactory to the Persons having the Direction of the Schools. No religious tracts will be used in the Schools, but such as are contained in the Catalogue of the SOCIETY FOR PROMOTING CHRISTIAN KNOWLEDGE. Annual or other communications on the state and progress will be made according to the custom of the Society.

At the same time (January 1839), Markland Barnard applied for financial aid from the National Society towards the construction of a schoolroom 40 feet long x 18 feet wide with an 11 feet high ceiling providing accommodation for 30 boys, 50 girls and 40 infants. The building costs were estimated to be:

Ground	£20
Building Labour & Materials	£186
Fitting-out	£30
Total	£236

London Colney History Society

1839 school room (left)
Teacher's House (right)

Annual costs running costs were estimated at £50 '*to be supported by a Personal Endowment of £20 from the Countess Dowager of Hardwicke, Subscription from Mr Oddie & the Incumbent & 1d [0.5p] weekly from each child...paid by the Parents*'.

After a donation of £100 from the Earl of Caledon together with £35 raised by other subscriptions there was a deficit of £101 to be raised and the application form is endorsed '*The Bishop of London spoke of the case and approved it*'. The school was built and the survey of land ownership and occupation in London Colney undertaken in 1840 for the purposes of the 1836 Tithe Commutation Act records that an area of '*24 perches*' owned by the '*Countess of Caledon*' was in use as '*School and premises*'.

A Visitation Return of 1842[3] completed by the minister, Markland Barnard, refers to the school having 90 pupils and comments that '*there are only 3 families who do not avail themselves of the National School*'; also reporting that '*I catechize the School children weekly*'. In 1848 William Upton, a Baptist minister in St Albans, published a survey of places of worship and schools in Hertfordshire which makes reference to the '*London Colney National and Sunday School for Boys and Girls...average attendance 100*' and

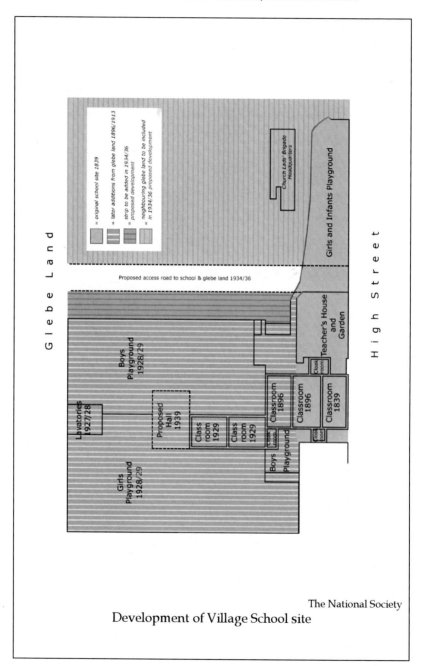

The National Society

Development of Village School site

comments that the school received children from a Dame school in Ridge. A lending library was operated from the school (later to be housed in the vicarage) and the survey records that *'Lady Caledon takes an active interest in the School at London Colney and supports the library'*. A Teacher's House adjoined the school and over the first 70 years 3 resident schoolmasters are recorded in the decennial census (for which they often acted as enumerators); Henry Hyde, Isaac Lloyd and John Birch. Henry Hyde described himself as a *'Church of England Schoolmaster'* (1851 census) and John Birch was a *'Schoolmaster and Organist'* (1891 census).

A further contribution to the funding of the school was made by the Dowager Countess of Hardwicke in 1850 when a gift of £799 invested in 3% Consols (government bonds) was placed in trust (Hardwicke Trust Fund) with the income to be used *'For the benefit of the Teachers in London Colney School'*[4]. James, 3rd Earl of Caledon, Catherine, Dowager Countess of Caledon, Georgina Oddie and Markham Barnard (*'Incumbent of the Chapel at London Colney'*) were the first trustees of the fund. Provision was made in the trust deed that future appointments to trusteeship should comprise the *'Owner or Occupier for the time being of Tittenhanger House aforesaid another of them shall be the Incumbent for the time being of the Chapel at London Colney aforesaid and the remaining Trustees shall be Gentlemen resident within 5 miles of Tittenhanger House aforesaid'*.

Over time the school premises were expanded[5] and encroached onto the glebe land. In 1896 a *'Portion of School & offices [were] built'* on part of the adjoining land and a further 2 classrooms were added. Later, in 1913 a further plot extending to ⅓ acre was leased to the School Managers for 50 years at a nominal yearly rent of £1. By 1924 the school comprised *'3 parallel rooms, each 36 feet long and 18 feet wide with two valleys in the roof'* and the Teacher's House. The report of the National Society's inspector in 1924, however, was critical of the facilities provided commenting that *'One room used at present by the infants is alongside the main London to Liverpool road passing through St Albans. This road is extensively used by fast and slow motor traffic so the room is noisy and if the roadside windows are open the teaching is considerably interrupted. If the windows are kept closed the ventilation suffers'*. He recommended that additional accommodation be built *'further back from the road'* and that the *'disused room will make an excellent hall for school assembly, for combined singing lessons and for physical exercises when the weather is unsuitable for outdoor work.'* Other criticisms included the ventilation and heating of the classrooms, inadequate size of the boys' playground and the report recommended that *'the offices [lavatories] will have to be reconstructed'* because:

> They are too few in number, too near the school premises and as they are on the pit system they are rather offensive. It is understood that a drainage system will shortly be introduced into Colney. If the Local Authority can give an approximate date when this work will be completed, it would be advisable for the Managers to delay this part of the improvements and then when all is ready, they could erect new offices fitted with flushing tanks and water supply and connect them with the drainage system.

Following the report the school managers set about raising finance in order to implement the recommendations but completion of the improvements was delayed. A significant contribution towards the costs was anticipated from the realisation of the assets of the Hardwicke Trust (£423) which, at that time, were controlled by the Board of Education but although negotiations were commenced in 1924 it was not until May 1929 that the Board approved the scheme for transfer of the capital. In the meantime, with funds raised by personal subscription (£214), proceeds from bazaars and jumble sales (£294) and a grant from the Voluntary Schools Association (£45), it was decided to proceed with the alterations and improvements to the existing premises before the construction of the additional classrooms. Work progressed in sections during 1927-1928 as funds became available. In addition to the alterations (£84), new lavatories were provided (£321) and the leased glebe land was purchased from the Ecclesiastical Commissioners (£50) upon which the new playgrounds were to be laid out (£50).

The delay in commencing construction of the additional classrooms created further complications. Firstly, the originally estimated sum of £650 increased to a contract price of £955 and, further, the proposed grant of £150 from the National Society was reduced to £60 because of a deterioration in its finances. Total costs of the building works together with other associated costs such as legal and architects fees amounted to £1089. The opportunity also was taken regularise the ownership of the original school site upon which stood the original classroom, the Teacher's house and part of the later additions. By a Deed of Gift of 14 May 1927 Elizabeth, Dowager Countess of Caledon, widow of the 4th Earl, transferred the property to the vicar and churchwardens of St Peter's Church, London Colney, as Trustees and Foundation Managers of the school but stipulated that should the land and premises *'not be used as a School or School House...for the space of one year'* the property would revert to the Caledon Trusts.

The following decade was a period of uncertainty for the school beginning with the departure of the headmaster, James Woolfall. London Colney County Council School (senior school) in Alexander Road opened on 5 January 1932 and an earlier arrangement recorded in the manager's minutes for September 1931 that *'when the present Headmaster of the London Colney C.E. [Church of England] School was appointed in 1926 he would be offered the headmastership of the new Senior School when opened'* was duly implemented[6]. By December 1932 the headmaster had left the Teacher's House which was subsequently used as an office, for medical inspections by the District Nurse and as a storeroom. Despite the improvements carried out in 1927-1929, nonetheless, the premises remained unsuitable and a report prepared in 1935 commented that the original classrooms were in a bad state of repair with *'dry rot and defective roofs...the Playground...was dusty in dry weather and very muddy in wet'*; the Teacher's House *'was uninhabitable...[and] since the time of Mr Birch some 45 years ago...there has been dampness in the walls of the Living Rooms...[and] there is no inside convenience'*. A radical solution was proposed under which the original school site and neighbouring glebe land fronting the High Street would be sold for development and a scheme introduced *'...by which additions are to be made to two classrooms erected about 1929 so that in effect a new school comprising six classrooms and a Hall in all, will be built at right angles to the road and not facing it'*. A new roadway was to provide access to the school and glebe land beyond with a strip of land alongside the roadway added to the school site.

The plans, however, soon ran into difficulties. A purchaser was found who was prepared to develop the site offered for sale and an application was made to the National Society for a grant towards the new school buildings but the Countess of Caledon blocked the scheme *'...by putting forward a claim that the Teacher's House has reverted to her'* under the terms of the Deed of 14 May 1927 because it would no longer be used for school purposes. The matter dragged on for some years and in 1936, on the advice of its solicitors, the National Society obtained Counsel's opinion which advised that the reverter clause in the deed was invalid and that under the Schools Sites Acts the claim for reversion was not well founded. Applications for a grant towards the rebuilding costs were submitted to the National Society in 1934 and again in 1936 but although the Dowager Countess did not obtain legal advice or seek to further her claim, nevertheless, her actions blighted the proposed development because the prospective purchaser was not prepared to risk the possibility of litigation and neither the sale nor the proposed school project proceeded. Cancellation of the additional classrooms caused overcrowding at the school and classes were held in a corrugated iron building that had been erected in 1900 on the neighbouring glebe land for the Church Lads' Brigade.

Events began to overtake the viability of the Church School. The local Board of Education took the decision to erect a junior school for 350 pupils in Alexander Road close to the senior school and Hertfordshire Education Committee recommended that the accommodation be increased to cater for an intake of infants because of the uncertainty surrounding the future of the Church School[7]. The new school was opened in 1939 although the Church School continued to provide nursery and infant facilities. For their part, in the same year, the managers of the Church School sought to implement an alternative strategy by proposing that the existing classrooms be reconditioned and a school hall sufficient to accommodate 300 infants be built adjoining the classrooms erected in 1929. Not only did the outbreak of the 2nd World War intervene to delay the proposal but within a few years the provisions of the proposed Education Act of 1944 caused the operation of church schools to come under close scrutiny. The Dean of St Albans Diocese commented in a letter of October 1943[8]:

> The Group Managers of the Church Schools in St Albans have been considering the problem of meeting the claims that will be made on the Church schools under the provisions of the forthcoming Education Bill. As you will know, the policy of the National Society and this Diocese is to keep as many schools under the control of the Church as is possible, and if the proposals for Aided Schools are

Ken Barker

2010 Site of Village School

enacted the Managers will have to find 50 per cent of the cost. This may mean in many localities that some schools will be lost or become controlled Schools and that Church people who are determined to keep Church Schools in the national system and to continue their special and most valuable tradition in English education will be obliged to pool their resources and think rather of the Church as a whole than of parochial limits and boundaries....The Junior Schools...are in a more precarious position.

After the war a decision was taken to close the school and at a meeting of the managers, under the chairmanship of John Booty, minister of St Peter's Church, London Colney, held on 18 July 1949 a resolution was passed *'to notify HCC [Hertfordshire County Council] that this School of St Peters London Colney would cease to function as a Church School on 29 July 1949'*[9]. On the day of closure the headmistress made a poignant final entry in the school Log Book[10]:

> Mr Avery sent to collect the gas stove which is his and only lent for the Church School's needs.
> Today this old school will cease to exist as a Church School. The 5 + children will be absorbed in the Junior School with Mr Pullen, Head Master, and the 5 − children will remain at home.

Mr Kerridge will be retained as Caretaker but Mrs Kerridge the
cleaner-helper will be given a fortnight's notice.
This concludes my service here.
H R Dingwell

The school managers permitted limited use of 2 classrooms in
order to ease overcrowding at the junior school and upon
termination of the arrangement part of the building was let to the
Fellowship Printing Service Ltd with the remainder utilised as the
parish hall[11]. In 1961 the site was acquired by St Albans Rural
District Council from the Church Commissioners and sold to R J
Gray Distributors Ltd, wholesale stationers of Borehamwood, in
1978[12]. Developed with warehousing the former school site at 72
High Street, London Colney, in 2010 is occupied by Infotec, an
office equipment supplier.

End notes
Unless otherwise stated the information with regard to the history of the school is
taken from the papers held by the Church of England Record Centre under
reference NS/7/1/3372
[1] CERC: Visitation Return 1834 FP Blomfield 71 ff29-30
[2] CA: Conveyance 26 July 1843
[3] CERC: Visitation Return FP Blomfield 72 f 169
[4] HALS: Trust Deed D/ECd/Q2
[5] HALS: Terriers DP93B/3/8 & remainder of paragraph.
[6] HALS: London Colney County Council School Minutes 23 September 1931
HED1/52/1
[7] *Herts Advertiser* 16 July 1937
[8] HALS: Letter HED1/51/1
[9] HALS: Minutes HED1/51/1
[10] HALS: ibid
[11] HALS: Terrier DP93B/3/8
[12] HM Land Registry HD221869

CHAPTER TWELVE

The Future

If there is a common strand flowing through the history of St Peter's Church it is the efforts of successive generations of clergy and parishioners to maintain and adapt the church in order to meet changing needs. During the preparation of this book another instalment in that history was being planned. In recent years it was recognised that radical works were required not only for essential maintenance but also to improve accommodation for the congregation. The minister, Lynne Fawns, explained:

> ...our church is...not managing to respond to the demands of a post modern generation and its needs. The 20 year old heating system failed last winter [2008], a rewiring is due and the present electrical set-up is not adequate, the floor is beginning to fail in some areas, and we are told we have dry rot under the floor. This is in addition to the fact that parts of the ceiling have started to crack. Perhaps even worse is the fact that we cannot accommodate anyone in a wheelchair in the main body of the church unless they are physically lifted into a pew....Furthermore, we have families with young children in buggies who cannot be kept in church because of the very small aisles and the buggies pose a hazard if left in the small foyer at the back of the church, should we need to evacuate the church in event of fire...We most definitely are not offering hospitality or allowing people their dignity.

Re-ordering of the church and the manner in which a more welcoming environment could be created were the major considerations. In 2007 a Feasibility Study Group was formed in order to consider the range of options available and a tour was made of several Hertfordshire churches where similar alterations had been undertaken. The findings of the Group were considered by the Parochial Church Council and a decision was taken to proceed with the selected options for improvements and repairs.

The most significant proposals were the removal of the narthex screen and erection of a glazed entrance lobby together with replacement of the pews in the chancel with chairs in order to provide more flexible seating arrangements. Architects, Michael Dales Partnership Ltd, were appointed and further discussion ensued in order to identify those tasks that could be performed by

Michael Dales Partnership

2010 Computer generated image of proposed changes to church

Michael Dales Partnership

2010 Computer generated image of proposed changes to church

Ken Barker

2010 Church cleared ready for contractors

volunteers and the alterations requiring specialist contractors.

Progress of the work was planned in 3 phases:

Phase 1
Renewal of the heating system

Phase 2
Laying insulation over the church ceiling.
Lifting and repair to flooring as required.
Levelling of floor over whole of church and building a new and extended altar dais.
Moving the font to the north-west (*ec* east) end of the church.
Removing the entrance lobby (narthex) at the south-east (*ec* west) end of the church.
Erection of a glass screen to form a smaller lobby.
Modification of electric wiring and lighting as necessary
Removal of existing pews in chancel and replacement with chairs.

Phase 3
Demolition of the link between the church and parish centre.
Provision toilet for the disabled in the parish centre.
Installation of glazed double doors between link and church.

A vigorous programme of fund raising was organised which would have been readily recognised by Thomas Newcome the original promoter of the church almost 200 years earlier. Special fund raising events were arranged, applications for grants were submitted and donations sought from private individuals and local businesses. Phase 1 of the work was implemented in March 2009 when the heating system was replaced and in February 2010 insulation of the roof was carried out by volunteers. After the morning service on Easter Sunday 2010 access to the church was closed and over the following 2 weeks teams of volunteers removed the flooring installed during the 1980 re-ordering (exposing the memorials in the chancel) and the narthex screen together with other preliminary works. The pulpit and pews no longer required were collected by architectural salvors. At the time of writing the arrival of contractors is awaited with the church planned to re-open in September 2010. In the interim the parish centre is, once again, being used for services.

Geoff Eldridge

Congregation gathered outside St Peter's Church
after Easter Sunday service 4 April 2010

Appendix One

In June 1823 the Reverend John Briggs, vicar of St Peter's Church (St Albans), wrote to the Church Building Society supporting the establishment of a chapel of ease at London Colney[1].

Eton College
Windsor
June 15 1823

Sir

Having just now been informed that the Society for promoting the Enlargement and Building of Churches and Chapels are to hold a monthly meeting tomorrow and contemplating the advanced state of the Summer. I think it expedient, at the hazard of some blame for the irregularity, and want of due preparation, to lay before the Society immediately some particulars of a Case in which their kind assistance, if it can be afforded, would be most useful and acceptable.

The Vicarage of Saint Peters, in the Town of St Albans, of which I am the Incumbent, is in the Diocese of London, and in the patronage of the Bishop of Ely; and I have authority from the Diocesan, and from the Patron, to say that they are ready to give their consent, on certain conditions, to the Erection of a Chapel at London Colney; a populous place; of which the greater part is in the said Parish and three miles and a half from the Mother Church; which moreover can afford no accommodation for its inhabitants; the remainder being in the Parish of Shenley and Diocese of Lincoln. Colney Heath, in St Peters Parish, is four miles from the Church and has a considerable population, scarcely within two miles of any Church. London Colney being on the high London Road, and full of Publick Houses, exposes its people to examples and temptations, which must necessarily cause the Sabbath to be Lamentably neglected, or spent in an indecent and disorderly manner – to say nothing of the general consequences, at all times, of the want of a place of Worship and a Resident Clergyman .

There is a Third Parish, that of Ridge, in the Diocese of London & Archdeaconry of St Albans; which has a small quantum of population, nearer by full three miles, to Colney, than to their own Church. I have taken pains to ascertain, to as great nicety as I can, the amount of that part of the population of my Parish which would be benefited by a Chapel at Colney; and find that they amounted, when the Census was taken in 1821, to 588. We may perhaps now safely put them at 630 and although I have not been able yet to procure an equally near and modern account of the population, similarly circumstanced, of Shenley and Ridge, I apprehend, from all that I can learn, that they will together with mine, somewhat exceed 1000. It has been suggested that we should, whether the Church Building Committee at Westminster be able, or not, to assist us with their Funds, avail ourselves of the Powers with which they are armed, to constitute parts of these three Parishes, within certain limits, an Ecclesiastical District, and a Chapelry; with the usual provisions according to the Act of 49 Geo: 3. But I cannot yet tell whether this is desired by the other Incumbents, or would be agreeable to the Patrons; although I am quite willing, on my own part, to consent to it.

I ought here to state, that my want of preparation on this point, and on the exact particulars of the population in Shenley & Ridge, as well as of the funds which we may expect to raise towards the building of a Chapel; arises simply from this cause – that the project, which was agitated, and failed, five years ago, has now suddenly been revived, by an opportunity having offered to secure a most eligible Site for a Chapel; which Site the Earl of Hardwicke who has property in my Parish and that part of Ridge (of which he is Patron) has just now bought, and kindly offers to give, for the said building.

I am aware, and have reminded his Lordship, that an Endowment will be necessary, before we can expect Consideration, or any Grant from Queen Anne's Bounty. But supposing an Endowment to be obtained, we shall need all the help that can, by urgent and extensive applications be procured, to defray the cost of the plainest building, capable of holding four or five hundred persons. There is, unfortunately, a heavy Church Rate levied at St Peters to pay Annuitants, who lent money 20 years ago for the re-building of the Church Tower and Chancel; and such generally, is the condition of the Inhabitants that nothing can be done Parochially. It is therefore on the ground of conjecture only that we look for private contributions to such an amount as to render the attempt practicable or prudent. It is, I understand, the more usual order, for Applicants first, to attempt to canvass for contributions, and to state what Subscriptions have been made, or promised, before they address themselves to your Society for any pecuniary assistance. But besides that the time is, for more than one reason, somewhat critical, I cannot help deliberately thinking that in our particular case – where the prospect is so vague and the Parish can do nothing by Rate, it would be an incitement to many who belong to it, to give something if they saw, in the powerful and respectable name of the Society for which you act, some encouragement and hope of accomplishing our arduous object. If even one Publick Institution, after the consent of the Patron and Diocesan should have been made known, were to sanction the undertaking and to put it in motion, by pledging themselves, on certain conditions, and at the proper period, to support it with a Donation; I am persuaded that our progress would be much more brisk and effectual. I am not yet prepared with an Estimate of the proportion of Free Sittings that we could offer; but it would certainly be considerable compared with the Pews that would be required and for which payment would willingly be made.

I beg pardon for the unreasonable length of this letter; which I have been obliged to write very hastily, as the topics occurred, without having time to reduce them to a more compact form. In consideration, however, I take the liberty to make it my earnest request, on behalf of the Incumbents, and much of the Inhabitants of each of these Parishes as the scheme would benefit; that, if it be consistent with the regulations and with the means of your Society, to launch us forth and swell our sails with their help and favour, they will the goodness to do so; and to announce it to me for encouragement of the many who will be solicited to embark in the same enterprise. I must not forget to apologise for omitting to use the customary printed form in which applications are made to the Society. The newness and suddenness of the revival of this project in question, just at the moment also of my removal to this place for three months, must plead my excuse for this informality – and for my expatiating as I have done.

I have the honour to be, Sir,
Your most obedient
humble Servant
John Briggs

---

[1]LPL: Grant correspondence ICBS 00463

Appendix Two

Letter from Reverend Thomas Newcome published in *The British Magazine & Monthly Register of Religious and Ecclesiastical Information* 1834 Vol III p 652

STEPS TO BE TAKEN IN BUILDING A CHURCH.

DEAR SIR, — The querist signing himself a "Lay Subscriber," in your 33rd Number, may, perhaps, think the following pieces of advice worth his attention, in proceeding "to raise a humble temple to God" in his deserted and godless village, coming as they do from one who has had as much experience of the difficulties and impediments that beset his path as any *country* parson *ever had*. His first query is – "To whom he should *first* apply? To the incumbent, or to the diocesan, or to whom?" To the incumbent before the bishop, for although incumbents have now less power of obstructing the design than they had formerly, (some ten years since, when I was concerned in this matter) yet no bishop will consent without previously knowing and duly considering the incumbent's sentiments on the matter. He will not set up altar against altar, nor doctrine against doctrine, nor *doctor against doctor;* curate *perpetual* against the lawful pastor of every soul within the precincts of his cure, without very strong and manifest reason. Sir William Scott (now Lord Stowell)[1] advised me, an incumbent and patron, against parting with the patronage of the chapel I was intending to build within my own *parish,* (but as much *for* the use of two more parishes as mine) and accordingly I was willing to undertake the duty without endowment, rather than incur the risk of annoyance. The endowment required by Bishop Pretyman[2] was only £40 per annum. I applied *first* to Lord Hardwicke, the patron of one parish[3], and impropriator of tithes in the other two parishes; and this real *noble* man at once offered to secure such endowment, if I would transfer the site of the intended chapel one hundred yards distance. I still hesitated, notwithstanding such tempting and generous offer, for this would bring upon me the necessity of consulting two more bishops and another incumbent — viz., the Bishop of London (our present admirable metropolitan)[4] the Bishop of Ely[5], the patron of the Peculiar — and of my friend, and ultimately *most* hearty colleague and coadjutor, the Rev. John Briggs, Fellow of Eton College, and then incumbent of St. Peter's [St Albans]. The tenant of the site which Lord Hardwicke was willing to have granted within my parish, was a *stiffish* dissenter, and though he gave me fifty shillings subscription[6], yet he would not give up a quarter of an acre of land, and fairly told me, "that a church within fifty yards of the front of his farm-house would annoy him as much as a meeting-house would annoy me at the end of my parsonage-garden!" I could not get any other eligible site within my own parish, all the land being *copyhold;* and if it had been freehold, there was not one Araunah[7] in the village that would have "freely" given land—no, nor even a yoke from off his ox or his horse's neck for such purpose—the tenants and householders being, in truth, almost all publicans, coach- masters and ostlers— "et hoc genus omne"[8].

Imprimis, then, your "Lay Subscriber" *should secure a site quietly,* or the price will be raised upon him. The donor, if such is found, may expect too much "consideration" other than pecuniary—perhaps to have an inordinately large pew, and gratis, too; whereas, if there be no endowment, every subscriber should be made distinctly to understand that so much space is reserved for free seats, and that so much per head must be paid for accommodation in seats not free, to constitute a fund (and a very precarious one too, "experto crede"[9]) for ordinary repairs, and clerk's salary, before any excess can be carried in aid of the endowment for the minister, if indeed he, poor man, has anything but his pew-rents to depend upon. Towns may by these alone support a minister as a bachelor, but how is your querist to make a *living* for his minister out of his 330 villagers, and may be a farmer or two, now selling his wheat at four or five shillings a bushel, and hopeless of paying rent, or *hopeful* of *not paying* tithe and church rates? I do not think that other parties will consent to your "Lay Subscriber's" opinion, that granting a site should carry patronage of the chapel along with it; but endowment also, I think, should do so, in a case like his—viz. a village, three miles from the parish church, and as many, probably, from the incumbent's glebe-house. If these hints shall be thought of any value, I will pursue the subject and sequel of my church-building history, and directions *for obtaining money,* that sine qua non, in a future Number of your Magazine; wishing, meanwhile, rather than hoping, that I may escape the suspicion of having written them as much to sing to my own praise and glory, like country psalm-singers, as for the benefit of your Layman correspondent.

End notes
[1] Lord Stowell (1745-1836) Judge of the High Court of Admiralty
[2] George Pretyman (1750-1827); Bishop of Lincoln 1787-1820; Parish of Shenley was in the Diocese of Lincoln
[3] Parish of Ridge
[4] St Peter's Church (St Albans) was in the Diocese of London
[5] The Bishop of Ely was the Patron of St Peter's Church (St Albans)
[6] There is no subscription of fifty shillings (£2.10.0) listed (see appendix 1)
[7] Araunah is the name given by the Books of Samuel to a member of a Canaanite tribe who owned the threshing floor on the summit of Mount Moriah that David purchased and used as the site for assembling an altar to God
[8] 'and everything of this kind'
[9] 'believe one who has had experience'

Appendix Three

Details of the subscriptions for the proposed chapel at London Colney were published in the County Herald and Weekly Advertiser on Saturday May 15 1824 and Saturday 24 December 1825. The lists of subscribers have been amalgamated (subscriptions that appeared in the second list are identified with *) and sorted alphabetically in order to provide a self-index.

	£	s	d
A Friend, St Albans	1	0	0
A Friend, ditto	2	0	0
Abel, Mr, London Colney	0	10	0
Ablett , Mr, St Albans	0	5	0
Alexander Esq. Henry, ditto	1	0	0
Allis, Mr James, ditto	0	7	0
Arnold, Mr, ditto	0	2	6
Avis, Mr, St Michael's	1	0	0
Bacon Esq. J N, St Albans, Alderman	2	2	0
Baker, Dr, St Peter's	1	1	0
Bakerfield, Mrs Elizabeth, St Albans	10	0	0
Ballard (postboy), Mr, ditto	0	2	6
Bankes, Captain, St Peter's	1	0	0
Barnes Esq. J M, ditto	40	0	0
Bayley, Rev Kennett, Sandridge, Herts	1	1	0
Beck, Mrs, London Colney	0	1	0
Bisney, Mr John, ditto	10	10	0
Boome, Mr Henry, ditto	21	0	0
Boys Esq. Edward, St Peter's	2	2	0
Brabant Esq. St Albans	2	2	0
Briggs, The Rev J, Vicar of St Peter's	25	0	0
Briggs, Rev John, to make £50*	25	0	0
Briggs, Mrs I, St Peter's	1	1	0
Briggs, Rev Thomas, Pattiswick, Essex	2	2	0
Brinder, Elizabeth and Mary Bayles	0	2	0
Brooks, Mr, St Albans	0	10	0
Brown, Mr, Abby Clerk, ditto	0	10	0
Brown, Mr Joseph, Parish Clerk, St Michael's	0	10	0
Brown Esq. James, St Peter's	30	0	0
Brown Esq. Wm, St Albans, Mayor	5	0	0
Browne, Rev Mr, Dissenting Minister, St Peter's	1	0	0

	£	s	d
Buckland, Mr, London Colney	1	1	0
Burgess Esq, surgeon, St Albans	1	0	0
Burr, Esq Dunstable*	5	0	0
Cane, Miss, St Albans	1	0	0
Canon Esq. William, East Hyde, Herts	5	0	0
Carter, Mr, weaver, St Albans	0	5	0
Carter, H M, Esq. Mayor of Hertford*	5	0	0
Chambers , Miss and Miss M Chambers, St Albans	5	0	0
Charles, Miss, ditto	1	0	0
Cherry, Mrs, St Michaels	1	0	0
Cherry, Mr Cherry, ditto	0	5	0
Clarke junior, Mr Thomas, St Peter's	0	10	6
Cole, Miss, St Albans	1	0	0
Constable, Mr, St Peter's	0	2	0
Cook, Mr, St Albans	0	1	0
Cooper, Mr, London Colney	1	1	0
Cosier, Mr, upholsterer, St Albans	0	5	0
Costin, Mr, London Colney	0	3	0
Cottle, Mr, at the Cock, St Albans	1	0	0
Cotton, Miss, St Peter's	5	0	0
Crouch, Mr, St Albans	0	1	0
Crowther, Mrs, St Peter's	1	0	0
Davies Esq. Warburton, Tittenhanger Green	25	0	0
Deayton, Mr, Town Hall, St Peter's	0	2	6
Deayton, Mr, Boot Inn, ditto	0	2	6
Deayton, Mr, Lamb, ditto	0	2	0
Devonshire, His Grace the Duke of*	25	0	0
Dickenson, Mr, London Colney	0	10	0
Dixon, Mr, St Albans	0	5	0
Domville Bart. Sir William, St Albans	10	0	0
Douton, Mr, auctioneer, Barnet*	1	0	0
Downing, Mr, St Peter's	0	2	0
Drayton, Mr John, St Albans	0	2	6
Durant Esq, E, High Cannons, Shenley	100	0	0
Ebbs, Mrs, London Colney	0	5	0
Edwards, Mr Henry, St Alban's Bank	1	1	0
Edwards, Mr George, St Albans	1	1	0
Ekins, Rev F, Morpeth	2	2	0
Ekins, Rear-Admiral C.B. Devon	2	2	0
Eling, Mr, St Albans	1	0	0

	£	s	d
Fairthorn Esq. Abbey Orchard, St Albans	1	0	0
Faithful, Rev J F, Rector of Hatfield	12	12	0
Fawel, Mr, St Albans	0	5	0
Fearnley Esq. Watford	10	0	0
Finch Mason Esq. Aldenham Lodge	10	10	0
Fisher, Miss, St Peter's	1	0	0
Fountain, Mr John, London Colney	1	1	0
Fowler, Mr Joseph, St Peter's	1	1	0
Fowler, Mr Benjamin, builder, ditto	1	0	0
Franks, William, Esq. Woodside, Herts	5	0	0
Fusedale, Mr, London Colney	0	2	6
G.P. St Peter's	1	0	0
Gape, Mrs, William ditto	10	0	0
Gape, Rev Charles, ditto	2	2	0
Garrett, Mr, London Colney	0	5	0
Gaussen, Mrs, Brookman's, Herts	30	0	0
Gaze, Mr, St Albans	1	0	0
Godbold, Mr, ditto	0	5	0
Gooch, Mr, St Peter's	0	5	0
Goodwin, Mr, Napsbury, Herts	1	1	0
Green, Mr, St Albans	0	5	0
Gregory, Mr, ditto	0	2	6
Grimston, The Hon. Misses*	20	0	0
Gutteridge, Mr, auctioneer, St Albans	5	5	0
Hadow Esq, Patrick, Colney House, High Sheriff	52	10	0
Hair, Mr, St Peter's	0	5	0
Hair, Wm, ditto	0	5	0
Hardwicke, The Earl of , for a site	157	10	0
Hardwicke, The Earl of, second subscription*	100	0	0
Hardwicke, The Earl of, for books, communion plate, hangings for pulpit, desk, and altar*	100	0	0
Harris, Mr Edward, auctioneer, Barnet*	1	0	0
Harwood, Mr, London Colney	[blank]		
Hawkins, Mrs, ditto	5	5	0
Haycock, Mr, St Albans	0	2	6
Heygate M.P. Alderman, North Mimms Place	100	0	0
Hill, Mr, stonemason, Barnet*	1	0	0
Hillyard, Mr, St Michael's	0	2	6
Hilton, Mr, London Colney	0	2	6
Holished, Mr, St Michael's	0	10	0

	£	s	d
House, Mr, draper, St Albans	0	2	6
Howard Esq. Thomas, St Michael's	5	0	0
Hudson, Mr, St Albans	0	1	0
Hughes, Rev Dr, Canon Residentiary of St Paul's	21	0	0
Hughes, Mrs, London Colney	0	1	0
Jaques Esq. John, ditto	21	0	0
Janes, Mr Thomas, ditto	1	1	0
Jefferson, The Rev Jacob, Vicar of Ridge	20	0	0
Johnson, Mrs, St Albans	0	1	0
Johnson, Mr, ditto	1	0	0
Jones, Mr Thomas, St Michael's	0	10	0
Jones Esq. Samuel, Dalton's, St Peter's	20	0	0
Jones M.P. Captain Charles, Bath	1	0	0
Kent, Mr, glazier &c, St Albans	1	1	0
Kentish, Mr, St Peter's	0	4	0
Kentish Esq. Joshua, ditto	1	0	0
Kentish Esq. William, ditto	1	0	0
Kilby, Mr, St Albans	2	2	0
Kingston Esq. ditto	1	1	0
Lamb Bart. Sir James	50	0	0
Langley, Mr, bookseller, St Albans	1	1	0
Langridge, Mr, St Peter's	1	1	0
Lewin, Mr, St Albans	5	0	0
Lipscomb Esq, I T, surgeon, ditto	1	1	0
Lord, Mrs, London Colney	0	5	0
Lord, Mr, ditto	1	1	0
Marston, Mr, St Albans	0	5	0
Martineau Esq. Peter, Bank, ditto	10	10	0
Mason, Mr John, ditto	5	0	0
Mason, Captain, R.N.*	5	0	0
Massey, Mr, St Albans	0	10	0
Mather Esq. John, St Peter's	5	5	0
Mather jun, John, Mrs Hawkins, St Albans	10	0	0
Mayborough, Lord, Tittenhanger House	10	0	0
Miller, Mr, upholsterer, St Albans	0	5	0
Mitchell, Mr, St Peter's	0	5	0
Moreton, Mrs, ditto	0	10	0
Munday, Mr, upholsterer, St Albans	1	1	0
Munday, Mr, George-street	0	2	6

	£	s	d
Nares, Esq. J. P. Napsbury*	10	10	0
Nash, Mr, bookseller, St Albans	0	5	0
Newcome, Miss, North Wales*	5	0	0
Newcome, Rev Richard, Warden of Ruthin	5	0	0
Newcome, The Rev Thomas, Rector of Shenley	65	0	0
Newcome, The Rev Thomas, second subscription to make £100*	35	0	0
Newcome, The Rev Thomas - Mr. Mears, the bellfounder's bill*	16	16	0
Nicholls, Mr Robert, auctioneer, St Albans	1	1	0
Nicholls, Mr James, ditto	1	0	0
Nicholson, Rev N, ditto	5	5	0
Osborn, Mrs, St Peter's	0	2	0
Osborne, Mrs, ditto	2	2	0
Pain, Mr James, Clerk of St Peter's Church	1	1	0
Peppercorn, Mr, St Peter's	0	5	0
Peters, Miss, Gresford, Denbighshire	1	0	0
Pew, Mr Eli, St Peter's	1	0	0
Pierepont, The Hon Henry, Tittenhanger*	10	10	0
Piggott Esq. Isaac, St Albans	1	1	0
Pollard, Mrs, St Peter's	0	5	0
Portens, Esq. Thomas, Colney Street*	5	0	0
Potter, Mr, St Albans	0	1	0
Powell, Rev H, East Thornden, Essex	2	2	0
Powell, Mr, St Peter's	0	10	0
Pridmore, Mr, London Colney	1	1	0
Pryor, Mr William, ditto	10	0	0
Reid Esq. John, Holywell House, Mrs Hawkins, ditto	10	10	0
Richards, Mr, St Peter's	0	10	6
Ridley Esq, G J, surgeon, St Albans	1	0	0
Rogers, Mr Joseph, Parish Clerk of Shenley	1	1	0
Rogers, Mr William, London Colney	1	1	0
Rolfe, Mr, St Albans	1	0	0
Round Esq. Henry	1	1	0
Rumball, Mr, land surveyor, St Peter's	1	0	0
Salisbury, The Marquis of	50	0	0
Saunders, Mrs, St Peter's	0	10	0

	£	s	d
Saunders, Mr, St Michael's	1	0	0
Scott Esq M.P. James, Rotherfield, Hants	10	10	0
Seabrook, Mr, St Albans	0	2	6
Sear, Mrs, St Peter's	0	2	6
Searanke Esq. Francis Carter, Waltham Cross	1	0	0
Searanke Esq. Francis Carter, St Albans	1	1	0
Sewell, Mr, ditto	1	0	0
Sharpe, Mrs, Clare Hall, Herts	5	0	0
Sharpe, Rev Andrew, Bamborough	5	0	0
Shirley, Mr Thomas, Salisbury*	5	0	0
Small, Rev Henry, Abbey	5	5	0
Small, Mrs	3	3	0
Smith, Mr, painter, St Peter's	1	0	0
Smith, Mr, St Peter's Academy	0	5	0
Smith, Mr, Sopwell Mill	0	5	0
Smith, Mrs, Woolpack Inn, St Albans	0	2	6
Smith, Mr James, St Peter's	0	2	6
Smith, Mr, painter, ditto	1	0	0
Smith Esq. George, architect, by professional services and journeys, gratis*	120	0	0
Smith Esq. M.P. Christopher	5	5	0
Smithers, Mr, St Peter's	0	5	0
Smorthwaite, Messrs, St Peter's	2	0	0
Smorthwaite, Messrs, ditto	2	0	0
Smorthwaite, Mr Reginald, St Albans	0	5	0
Snell, The Rev Thomas, Salisbury Hall*	25	0	0
Society for the Enlargement and Building of Churches	400	0	0
Society for the Enlargement and Building of Churches*	100	0	0
Spencer, Mrs, London Colney	0	2	6
Story Esq. J, S St Albans	[blank]		
Story Esq. J S, law services, gratis*	20	0	0
Tebboth, Mr Thomas, Shenley	1	1	0
Tebboth (at the Trumpet), Mr, St Albans	0	5	0
Thompson, Seth, St Peter's	25	0	0
Thompson, Mr, ditto	0	2	0
Timperon, Joseph Esq. New Barnes	30	0	0
Trimmer, Miss Sarah, Brentford Butts	20	0	0
Trinder Esq. John, Shenley	1	1	0
Verulam, The Earl of	50	0	0
Wagstaff, Mrs, Wood Hill, Shenley	5	0	0

	£	s	d
Ward, Mr, St Peter's	0	10	0
Ward, Mr, St Albans	0	5	0
Watson, The Rev Dr, Archdeacon of St Albans	31	10	0
Watson, Mr David, St Peter's	1	1	0
Webster Esq, Richard, surgeon, St Albans	1	1	0
Wellingham, Mr, ditto	1	0	0
West Esq. Richard ditto	1	0	0
White, Mr, draper, Barnet*	0	10	6
Wigg Esq. John, Park Street, Herts	20	0	0
Wildboar, Mr, St Peter's	1	1	0
Wilde, Mr, St Albans	5	0	0
Wilkes, Mr, St Peter's	0	2	6
Wilkins, Mr, coachmaker, St Albans	0	10	6
Wilson M.P. Sir Henry Wright	5	5	0
Winter Esq. J Mico, Shenley*	21	0	0
Woodhouse, Mr, St Albans	0	5	0
Woollen Esq. Charles, ditto	21	0	0
Young, Mr, St Peter's	0	5	0

Appendix Four

Organ built by Hill & Son 1865 situated in the NE corner of Nave

Action: Tracker

Manual (C - g3, 56 notes):

Open Diapason	8 ft	
Stopped Diapason	8 ft	(lowest octave only)
Stopped Diapason Treble	8 ft	(from tenor C)
Claribel (a tapered Gamba)	8 ft	(from tenor C)
Dulciana	8 ft	(from tenor C)
Principal	4 ft	
Wald Flute	4 ft	
Fifteenth	2 ft	
Cornopean	8 ft	

Pedal (CC – G, 20 notes):

Bourdon   16 ft

Pedalboard:

Straight and flat

All pipework enclosed except Open Diapason and Bourdon

Accessories;

Hitch-down swell pedal (closed/half-open/open positions)
2 Composition pedals to manual stops
2 Composition pedals for manual-to-pedal coupler

Index

NB Index does not include the names of subscribers listed in Appendix 3.